KU-211-977

CUNARD

THE MOST FAMOUS OCEAN LINERS IN THE WORLD™

Mortification

Mortification

Writers' Stories of Their Public Shame

EDITED BY ROBIN ROBERTSON

FOURTH ESTATE · *London* and *New York*

First published in Great Britain in 2003 by
Fourth Estate
An imprint of HarperCollins*Publishers*
77–85 Fulham Palace Road,
London W6 8JB
www.4thestate.com

9 8 7 6 5 4 3 2 1

A catalogue record for this book is available from the
British Library

ISBN 0-00-717137-4

Typeset by Rowland Phototypesetting Limited,
Bury St Edmunds, Suffolk.

Printed in Great Britain by
Clays Ltd, St Ives plc

to Ramona

'The first prerogative of an artist in any medium
is to make a fool of himself.'

Pauline Kael

'We are all strong enough to bear the misfortunes
of others.'

François La Rochefoucauld

Preface

I can date, with some precision, the genesis of this project. It was midwinter in Manchester; a cold, wet November evening many years ago. The audience in the city-centre bookshop was unusually small, but I bravely attributed this to the big match being played that night at Old Trafford. Two poems into my reading I looked up confidently, over the heads of the half-dozen, and saw, being pressed flatly against the plate-glass, a pair of huge white buttocks. Then a second. Then the rest of the back four. It is hard to regain one's composure after being mooned at by a passing group of United supporters – particularly when they begin to outnumber the audience.

Humiliation is not, of course, unique to writers. However, the world of letters does seem to offer a near-perfect micro-climate for embarrassment and shame. There is something about the conjunction of high-mindedness and low income that is inherently comic; something about the presentation of deeply private thoughts – carefully worked and honed into art over the years – to a public audience of strangers, that strays perilously close to tragedy. It is entirely possible, I believe, to reverse Auden's dictum that 'art is born out of humiliation'.

Having spent many years in the company of writers before and after public engagements, I have been regularly entertained by their tales of past deflations, and struck by their willingness to turn abasement into anecdote. These are the best stories, I think: those told against the teller. And for the reader, apart from the sheer *schadenfreude* of it all, there is admiration too: for that acknowledgement of human frailty, of punctured pride, but also of the seeming absurdity of trying to bring private art into the public space.

Many of the stories collected in this book concern the audience (or, more commonly, the lack of one), fellow readers, the organizer, the venue, the 'hospitality', or the often interminable journey there and back. Then there are the experiences of teaching and being taught, reviewing and being reviewed, of festivals, panel discussions, symposia, signing sessions, literary parties and prizes, and the trips abroad, with all the attendant joys of translation. Finally there are also the forays into other media – particularly the bright worlds of television and radio – that can bring so many more people to share in your shame. Grief's handmaiden through all this, it need hardly be said, is alcohol – in all varieties but only one size: *too much*. Drink courses through these pages like a Biblical flood.

Despite inviting as many women as men to join this grim celebration, there is a distinct preponderance of male writers. This did not come as a huge surprise: the statistics show that the male of the species is more prone to indignity – or more used, at least, to having his indignities displayed in public. The Scots and Irish are out in force, but those countries are – as I know to my cost – the very cradles of shame. Nor do I make any excuse for the high proportion of poets. The whole enterprise of writing poetry is a *de facto* folly. These people devote days to single lines and years to preparing each slim collection, and then publish their work into a yawning maw of indifference. The poet, as Baudelaire explains,

> 'is like the prince of the clouds,
> who rides the tempest and spurns the archer;
> exiled on the ground, amid scorn and derision,
> his giant wings prevent his walking.'

The wings, certainly, but also the three bottles of house white.

While there are occasional undercurrents of seriousness in these stories – a desire for something between expiation and exorcism, perhaps – their main intention is to make us laugh, while feeling a strong sense of 'there, but for the grace of God, go I'. It is greatly to the credit of all the contributors that they have embraced their mortification so warmly – returning to the scene of the crime and leading us, hot-faced, through their hell.

Acknowledgements

My grateful thanks go to the writers who agreed to open all these old wounds and generously take part in this second humiliation, and to those others I invited to contribute but who thought, quite sensibly, that once was more than enough.

I also want to thank my agent, Derek Johns, and my editor, Nicholas Pearson, for their encouragement and assistance.

Contents

'Futility: playing a harp before a buffalo.' Burmese proverb

Margaret Atwood

Mortifications never end. There is always a never-before-experienced one waiting just around the corner. As Scarlett O'Hara might have said, 'Tomorrow is another mortification.' Such anticipations give us hope: God isn't finished with us yet, because these things are sent to try us. I've never been entirely sure what that meant. Where there is blushing, there is life? Something like that.

While waiting for the mortifications yet to come, when I'll have dentures and they'll shoot out of my mouth on some august public occasion, or else I will topple off the podium or be sick on my presenter, I'll tell you of three mortifications past.

Early period
Long, long ago, when I was only twenty-nine and my first novel had just been published, I was living in Edmonton, Alberta, Canada. It was 1969. The Women's Movement had begun, in New York City, but it had not yet reached Edmonton, Alberta. It was November. It was freezing cold. I was freezing

cold, and I went about wearing a secondhand fur coat – musk-rat, I think – that I'd bought at the Salvation Army for $25. I also had a fur hat I'd made out of a rabbit shruggie – a shruggie was a sort of fur bolero – by deleting the arms and sewing up the armholes.

My publisher arranged my first-ever book signing. I was very excited. Once I'd peeled off the muskrats and rabbits, there I would be, inside the Hudson's Bay Company Department Store, where it was cozily warm – this in itself was exciting – with lines of eager, smiling readers waiting to purchase my book and have me scribble on it.

The signing was at a table set up in the Men's Sock and Underwear Department. I don't know what the thinking was behind this. There I sat, at lunch hour, smiling away, sur-rounded by piles of a novel called *The Edible Woman*. Men in overcoats and galoshes and toe rubbers and scarves and earmuffs passed by my table, intent on the purchase of boxer shorts. They looked at me, then at the title of my novel. Sub-dued panic broke out. There was the sound of a muffled stam-pede as dozens of galoshes and toe rubbers shuffled rapidly in the other direction.

I sold two copies.

Middle period
By this time I'd achieved a spoonful or two of notoriety, enough so that my US publisher could arrange to get me onto an American TV talk show. It was an afternoon show, which in those days – could it have been the late seventies? – meant variety. It was the sort of show at which they played pop music, and then you were supposed to sashay through a bead curtain, carrying your trained koala bear, or Japanese flower arrangement, or book.

I waited behind the bead curtain. There was an act on before me. It was a group from the Colostomy Association, who were talking about their colostomies, and about how to use the colostomy bag.

I knew I was doomed. No book could ever be that riveting. W.C. Fields vowed never to share the stage with a child or a dog; I can add to that, 'Never follow the Colostomy Association.' (Or any other thing having to do with frightening bodily items, such as the port-wine-stain removal technique that once preceded me in Australia.) The problem is, you lose all interest in yourself and your so-called 'work' – 'What did you say your name was? And tell us the plot of your book, just in a couple of sentences, please' – so immersed are you in picturing the gruesome intricacies of . . . but never mind.

Modern period
Recently I was on a TV show in Mexico. By this time I was famous, insofar as writers are, although perhaps not quite so famous in Mexico as in other places. This was the kind of show where they put make-up on you, and I had eyelashes that stood out like little black shelves.

The interviewer was a very smart man who had lived – as it turned out – only a few blocks from my house, in Toronto, when he'd been a student and I'd been elsewhere, being mortified at my first book signing in Edmonton. We went merrily along through the interview, chatting about world affairs and such, until he hit me with the F-question. The do-you-consider-yourself-a-feminist question. I lobbed the ball briskly back over the net ('Women are human beings, don't you agree?'), but then he blindsided me. It was the eyelashes: they were so thick I didn't see it coming.

'Do you consider yourself *feminine*?' he said.

Nice Canadian middle-aged women go all strange when asked this by Mexican talk-show hosts somewhat younger than themselves, or at least I did. 'What, at my age?' I blurted. Meaning: *I used to get asked this in 1969 as part of being mortified in Edmonton, and after thirty-four years I shouldn't have to keep on dealing with it!* But with eyelashes like that, what could I expect?

'Sure, why not?' he said.

I refrained from telling him why not. I did not say: *Geez Louise, I'm sixty-three and you still expect me to wear pink, with frills?* I did not say: *feminine, or feline, pal? Grr, meow.* I did not say: *This is a frivolous question.*

Whacking my eyelashes together, I said: 'You really shouldn't be asking *me*. You should be asking the men in my life.' (Implying there were hordes of them.) 'Just as I would ask the women in *your* life if you are masculine. They'd tell me the truth.'

Time for the commercial.

A couple of days later, still brooding on this theme, I said, in public, 'My boyfriends got bald and fat and then they died.' Then I said, 'That would make a good title for a short story.' Then I regretted having said both.

Some mortifications are, after all, self-inflicted.

'The dumbness in the eyes of animals is more touching than the speech of men, but the dumbness in the speech of men is more agonizing than the eyes of animals.' Hindustani proverb

Glyn Maxwell

The West Midlands, 1990

Library Lady: So. Excellent. Are there any questions for our poets? Yes? ... From anyone ... about anything ... *in* the, the, the poetry? We've heard today?

Really anything ...

Actually *I* – oh, yes?
Schoolgirl: Like to ask Glen Maxwell something.
Poet: Yep. Sure. Great.
Schoolgirl: That last poem.
Poet: 'Seventh Day'?
Schoolgirl: Yeah.

Poet:	What would you like to ask?
Schoolgirl:	Well. What's it about?
Poet:	What's the poem about?
Schoolgirl:	Yeah. What's it about?
Poet:	Hmm ... I suppose you could say it's about it's about it's about let's see. The speaker, or narrator, who may or may not be me, note ... well all right I suppose it is me but it doesn't necessarily *follow* it is anyway ... The narrator. Is. Someone who's woken up on a Sunday morning having obviously you know enjoyed himself wahay on the previous Saturday night if-ya-know-what-I-mean, I expect you do! so, right, so what I mean is is he's dealing with a hangover that's in the second stanza those are hangover cures or they're not, nothing is, at least *I* find. Sleep maybe. But you know what a hangover is, don't you, right yes, you do, of course ha ha, maybe you've got one now! maybe not, no of course, no. You haven't, you're you're 13. And I'm anyway fourth stanza. I haven't either of course, fourth stanza he's feeling sort of wired, sort of sensitive you could say, and he's suffering, he feels like he's got one skin less than you know, the average, er, skin allocation, and he cares what people say, that's an aspect certainly – *of* it. So he wanders around the house, sort of not engaging with this or that, feeling kind of existential – er ... feeling kind of like an existing you know *thing*, thinking about himself like in the universe, alone in it, with as I say, that skin thing,

from earlier. And the breathing, obviously. That regular, sort of, measure like a, I don't know, like a . . . listen. Can't hear it . . . And he what, I'm just checking it now he, he can't sleep, on top of all that he's lying there or sitting there and he can't sleep, he looks out of the window see in the middle of the eighth stanza, eighth *stanza* . . . *Stanza.* Italian for *room.* He's in a room, just as he's in a oh GOD . . .

Sorry, little sip of water, that's good, Volvic, so he looks out, away, off, out at his own town, which is you know, just like your own town, but it's my own town as opposed to, as opposed to . . . and he's there, there with his water, and he takes a you know a pill to sleep which ends his his his consciousness his awareness as it indeed it ends the poem at that very exact point because beyond it there's only the see for yourself the well the the the whiteness.

Schoolgirl: Why didn't you just write that then.

'There smites nothing so sharp, nor smelleth so sour
As shame.' Langland, *Piers Plowman*

Janice Galloway

My granny had no patience with books and writers. None at
all. A miner's widow, she had a glass eye (a coal explosion in
her own grate), a clay pipe (mostly unlit) and a habit of saying
out loud what you hoped she wouldn't. 'Away and work',
was a favourite *bon mot* for oblivious glass-screen TV
announcers; 'Is that smell you?' a witticism directed at door-
stepping Mormons; 'I've got my eye on you' whilst removing
the aforementioned glass appendage, the perfect remark to
drain the blood from the faces of small children – you know
the kind of thing. Years after she died in a house fire, my
mother, unwell herself, told me in the manner of it being a
last confession how much she had loved her mother, yet how
embarrassed by her she had been. Not just embarrassed,
marked. The worst, it seemed, needed to emerge.

As a teenager, maybe eighteen or nineteen, she had taken
her mother on a very rare, very special Big Night Out. The
dazzling first showing of *Gone with the Wind* was the occasion
in question, and women for miles had come in their fanciest

duds to sit in the dark and watch it. The local fleapit had been done up and paper hankies and specially drafted-in boxes of Milk Tray were available in the foyer. This was glamour indeed, and my mother was enthralled with all of it before the movie even started. By the time a daring onscreen clinch reduced the cinema to sex-tingled silence, she was rapt almost beyond recall. At the pitch of the silence, however, a man sitting next to my mother, possibly despite his best efforts, possibly from a surfeit of unaccustomed chocolate, broke wind. My granny jumped to her feet, grey bun outlined in the projection beam, roaring, 'It wasny me, it was him.' She roared it repeatedly, pointing. By the time they were asked to leave, my mother already had and my granny had started a fight with two usherettes. 'All those people,' my mother sighed. Forty-five years later, she still blushed at the memory, the loss of fragile, teenage dignity. 'She wasny what you'd call *graceful*.'

Twenty years later still, I have no idea what either my mother or grandmother would have made of my being a writer, and that's probably a damn good thing. I don't know what I make of it either. I do know it works best when I'm alone and it's when I haul myself in front of 'all those people' too that things seem more fraught. From the very first surreal radio interview, where I expected to be asked questions about the book I had just written and was instead asked by a ferociously chirpy Angela Rippon what I'd be doing to celebrate National Foot Week, this has been the case. It honestly never seems like me.

Book in hand, I have been introduced in Leeds as 'an up-and-coming comedienne from Billy Connolly country'. I have been heckled in Haworth as the organizer of a lesbian 'happening' about which I knew nothing, and had my invitation to a feminist conference in Motherwell rescinded on the grounds of being found out as 'not feminist enough'. I have been thrown out of Amman University for being unable to truthfully promise I would not use the word 'thighs' during my session on the platform, yet dismissed as roundly as if I had won the Bad Sex Award by the all-too-audible snoring of a blue-rinsed lady as I read what I had hoped would be a pretty in-your-face fellatio story. I have been offered, free, a 'cheerier ending' for that story about ECT I just narrated, and one rather timid-looking chap waited for over an hour in a queue to tell me, as I signed his book, that he only wanted to say how much he hated my stuff and, while he was at it, my fucking earrings as well. I have been booked into a posh, would-be chic hotel with such vile green lighting I got a headache almost at once, and off-loaded into a dimly-lit warren where the wallpaper peeled down the wall, where the holes in the skirting looked too big to have been made even by Scottie dogs, where the locks didn't work and the phone was disconnected and the local knocking-shop activity seemed set to begin at any second. I have even been asked if I minded not being paid.

Only once, though, at a reading in Edinburgh, have things almost come to a head. In the heart of a stillness I deliberately, and, I thought, dramatically, created, the bloke in the front row (at least I think it was the bloke in the front row) executed the loudest arse-raspberry I ever hope to hear. Maybe it was blood, maybe the poetry of repeated history suggesting itself. Whichever, in the space of a split-second, I found a horribly persuasive understanding with my long-dead Granny McBride. Some notion of personal dignity seemed to be at stake: the old lady's words were forming on my lips. In the same split-second, however, I recalled my son, aged ten, was watching from the back row of the audience. The sudden recollection of my mother's forty-five-year-long blush made the choice: there was nothing else for it. I struck a pose of transcendental deafness, unfocused my eyes, and carried, if not sublimely then at least determinedly, freshly, on.

Grace, you see. It's worth striving for.

I think my mother would have been proud.

'Every author, however modest, keeps a most outrageous vanity chained like a madman in the padded cell of his breast.'
Logan Pearsall Smith

Rupert Thomson

In the winter of 1992–1993 my girlfriend, Kate, and I went to live in La Casella, an isolated farmhouse some forty miles south-east of Siena. It was a good place to write, and I had the vague but oddly compelling feeling I always have when it's time to start work on a new novel. I was relieved to be out of London, partly because I wanted to avoid another grim English winter, and partly because I wanted to forget all about the 'Best Of Young British Novelists 1993', which was to be announced early in the New Year. By a strange coincidence, I had been staying in the same house exactly ten years before, when the 'Best Of Young British Novelists 1983' had been announced, and I had devoured that issue of *Granta*, eager to acquaint myself with a new generation of writers, writers whom I hoped one day to emulate. This time, though, I qualified: I had published two novels – *Dreams of Leaving* and *The Five Gates of Hell* – and I was not yet forty. People who moved in literary circles had told me that I might be on the list – some had even said I *should* be on the list – whereupon I would usually smile or shrug. I may have affected a certain indifference, but deep down, of course, I was *desperate* to be on the list. At the same time I felt fatalistic about the whole thing: I fully expected to be passed over, and I had no intention of being in London when that happened.

It was a great winter. Kate read novels and cooked goulash and went for long walks through the Tuscan countryside. I wrote. Some of our favourite people came to stay and we sat up late, drinking bottle after bottle of the colonel's red wine (he charged three thousand lire for two litres). One of the house rules was that I shouldn't be interrupted during working hours – unless, of course, there was some kind of emergency. I don't think we had any emergencies that winter, though, so I wasn't disturbed at all – not, that is, until a certain afternoon in early March. It must have been cold in the house that day because Kate had decided to light a fire. While tearing up strips of newspaper – neighbours would often pass papers on to us, though we rarely read them – her eye fell on a small black-and-white photograph of me. She scanned the article. The 'Best Of Young British Novelists 1993' had been announced the week before. She ran upstairs with the paper and burst into my room.

'You've been chosen,' she said. 'You're on the list.'

I turned to face her.

'You're one of the Best Young British Novelists,' she said.

'Really? Let me see.' My heart was racing.

We scanned the list of writers, but my name wasn't there. We scanned the list again. There was no mention of me at all.

'But your picture's here,' Kate said, her finger poised over one of the black-and-white mug shots. 'Look.'

We both looked. It wasn't me. It was Jeanette Winterson.

Neither of us spoke for a while.

'I'm sorry,' Kate said at last. She had turned away from me. She was facing into the corner of the room.

In retrospect, I suppose the photo did look vaguely like me – or like a *version* of me anyway (there must have been a time when Jeanette and I had a similar haircut, or perhaps we narrowed our eyes in the same way when we were looking into the sun). I stared and stared at the picture, as if the closeness of the resemblance could somehow lessen the hurt.

'I'm sorry,' Kate said again, then she went downstairs.

It was humiliating for both of us, of course – for Kate because she had mistaken Jeanette for me, and because she had raised my hopes only to dash them seconds later, but it was humiliating for me too – *especially* for me – because I had responded with such eagerness, such desperation, with such incontinent desire, all my ambition and longing exposed; I felt like someone who had been disembowelled and then left to stare dumbly at the brightly-coloured mess of his own intestines.

The days that followed were difficult. There was only one consolation that I could think of. The next time they chose the 'Best Of Young British Novelists', in 2003, I would be too old. I would never have to go through this again.

'You should punish your appetites rather than allow yourself to be punished by them.' Epictetus, *Fragments*

John Burnside

It's hard to think of an isolated instance of mortification that is worse, or more typical, or more mortifying than any other, since mortification seems to me the natural, and fairly predictable consequence of any public display of lyricism. Still, there are degrees of mortification (from Ecclesiastical Latin: *mortificare*, to kill or subdue), which may be classified thus:

1: Mild Form: Reading to any audience in a 'cabaret' setting (i.e. they're only there for the beer/wine/vodka mixers/cold sausage pies/raffle).

Optional variation: audience member vomits/passes out/dies halfway through the performance.

2: Persistent Form: Former lover turns up and sits brooding in front row throughout reading.

Optional variation: Former lover weeps/sniggers/bleeds in front row throughout reading.

3: Virulent Strain: Any award ceremony where the short-listed poets, ignorant as to the result that is about to be announced, are obliged to wait, in a roomful of their peers (and other hostile parties), while the sub-sub-minister for Sport, Leisure and the Creative Industries demonstrates his or her complete ignorance of anything even remotely related to poetry or the arts (including the name of the award, and the institution making it).

Optional variation: Announcement of the winning book/poem/project which is not one's own; c.f. Gore Vidal, 'Whenever a friend succeeds, a little something in me dies.'

Bewildering and occasionally fatal variation: Announcement of a winning book/poem/project that is not only not one's own, but transparently political/transparently autobiographical/absurdly technical/pure Home Service.

Its etymology notwithstanding, mortification is rarely fatal and is relatively short-lived. The usual treatment is stoicism and temporary withdrawal. In cases where mortification is suspected, the patient should on no account be offered, or allowed to partake of, alcohol.

'If we heard it said of Orientals that they habitually drank a liquor which went to their heads, deprived them of reason and made them vomit, we should say: How very barbarous!'
La Bruyère, *Of Opinions, Characters*

David Harsent

It's 1969 or '70, my first book is just out, and I've been asked by Alan Hancox to read at his bookshop in Cheltenham. Reading with me will be John Fuller, James Fenton and Peter Levi. John has offered to drive us all to Cheltenham from Oxford, so I get the bus to Oxford and arrive early to have a lunchtime beer with my friend Fred Taylor who is up at Keble. We get drunk. It's not difficult, but it is unexpected.

Being pissed, we do the logical thing and buy some bottles of wine to take back to Fred's flat in Botley (a deliberate socialist league or more from the dreaming spires). By mid-afternoon I am seriously confused but also happy and confident. Fred's a student so, of course, has no phone. I call John from a phone box to let him know that I am somewhere in Oxford and 'opposite a garage that looks like a cathedral'. Somehow or another, he tracks me down to where I am dozing on the kerb with my legs stretched out into the road and the traffic making little detours round me, and takes me back to his house. The others are already there. I accept a drink and sit on Peter Levi's glasses.

The drive to Cheltenham takes three or, maybe, four minutes and I spend the time with my head out of the window, like the family labrador. We get to Alan's shop where I accept a drink. The reading isn't scheduled to take place for an hour or more, so the plan is that we'll first go for an Indian meal, then read, then return to Alan's house for a bit of a party. All this sounds terrific to me, insofar as I can make sense of it. I nod and smile and accept a drink.

At the Indian restaurant I order most of what the menu has to offer, eat it, and clear up the residue of others' meals from the little dishes on the hot-plates. I've switched from wine back to beer, now, which seems a safe and sensible move. Somewhere a conversation is going on, of which I am a part. Somewhere else, a coracle is afloat on a dark and boisterous sea, myself adrift in that craft, but still happy and confident and anticipating safe landfall.

We return to the bookshop where an audience has assembled: people sitting on the floor in penumbral gloom. At the other end of the shop and, by contrast, under fierce lights, is a trestle table and four chairs. We read in alphabetical order, so Fenton, Fuller, Harsent . . . who (so far as I can judge) stands, reads, sits, perhaps even acknowledges the applause with a wry smile and a tilt of the head. Peter Levi then gets up to read and I go to sleep – instantly – as night falls on the veldt.

The next thing I know, I'm being woken by James because Alan Hancox has thanked the poets, but also called for a last poem from each of us. Okay, I'm slightly flustered now. In fact, I haven't a clue where in hell I am or where I've been. What I do suspect is that I didn't sleep silently. (I was given, in those days, to whimpering in my sleep, a characteristic that some girls claimed to find endearing; so much so, in fact, that

I had become pretty adept at faking sleep-and-whimper to make myself seem interesting and vulnerable.)

Faint sounds of a running sea give way to anticipatory applause. A reflexive response gets me to my feet. James is also standing, it being his turn to read. I sit. He sits. I stand again and fumble through the pages of my book, muttering that I don't know quite what to read. Peter Levi suggests I re-read the last poem from my set. Since I haven't the faintest idea what it was, he helps me find it, despite having trouble with his glasses which, I notice now, are badly bent and sitting askew on his nose. The poem he finds for me is the longest poem in the book. I assume this to be an act of sabotage, but can't find it in me to blame him.

I read it. I sit. James stands. I stand, too, not in error, but because it has suddenly been borne in upon me that I am about to be sick. Pretty soon. Any minute. In fact, about now. I come out from behind the trestle table as James begins to read, and plunge through the audience (all on the floor, all in semi-darkness) raising a small chorus of screams and yelps as I tread on fingers and kick shins. The lavatory is a little beyond the last row. I go in, I kneel, I experience that fractional pause, then I throw up.

There can, I know, be discreet upchucks of the cough-and-gob variety, or even the girlish whisper-and-slip. This is not either of those, nor is it the twenty-gauge-shuck-and-reload or even the storm-drain-rib-racker. No. This is *volcanic*. This is a fully-orchestrated, bass-pedal-active, hog-hollerin', bootsoles-to-bogbowl, ten-gallon tsunami.

I emerge, pale, shaky and still drunk, with (I've no doubt) all sorts of evidence of my recent activity on display. The imprint of the lavatory seat lugs on my forehead, for instance. Detritus. *Smearing*. That sort of thing. The lights in the shop are up. The poets are mingling with the audience. Drinks are on offer. I wonder vaguely whether my whimpering might have raised, in some blonde, slim, young, pretty member of the audience feelings of protectiveness and lust in equal measure. Or brunette, slim, young; or more or less any shade of reddish-brown, etc., etc. Steadied by the possibility, I accept a drink.

Later, we go to Alan's house for the promised party. I am destined to remember little of this, though I am aware of accepting several drinks and dancing with someone who seems slim, young and pretty and definitely has hair.

I wake next morning in the attic. I must have started out on that camp bed over there, but now I'm over here and feeling . . . well . . . okay, as it happens. Happy and confident, you might say. This lasts for several blissful seconds, before someone enters the room, stealthily, creeps up behind me, clubs me to the floor and stamps repeatedly on my head. It's my hangover saying 'Good morning'.

I have always thought it fair and reasonable that a hangover should be proportionate to the previous night's intake of booze to its behavioural excesses. It's a sin thing. You cut a deal with a vengeful God. This hangover, it seems to me, is way out of line. In fact, if it takes one more step towards lethality (being only a step-and-a-half away) it will probably be ordered to retreat and reform. Surely I can't deserve . . . Then grimy little scraps of last night's doings start to come together in my mind; tawdry sense-impressions; mucky images; an acrid smell. And I realise I must have earned the lot. In fact, I'm probably lucky to be standing upright. (Am I standing upright?) The only hope is that what I've so far remembered will be all memory serves up. Except I know it won't. That smell isn't mice in the wainscot or rot in the beams; it's the low, cloacal stench of humiliation and guilt.

I dress (which act poses certain questions) and go downstairs. No one's up. I make myself a cup of tea. I find the bathroom and throw up, not quite the whisper-and-slip I hope for, but not much more than a whoop-and-splatter. A little later, Alan appears, wearing a wide smile and takes me to breakfast at George's in the market, where I consume the full English morning-after cure and manage, against some odds, to hang on to it. Alan seems worryingly cheery, to say nothing of chatty and smiley. After the second egg, I can stand no more. I look at him through bruised eyeballs.

'Alan, I'm really sorry about last night.'

'What?'

'Last night. I'm sorry.'

'Last night what?'

'You must have noticed.'

'Noticed what?'

'I was drunk. I was drunk when I arrived. I was drunk in the Indian restaurant. I was drunk when I read. I threw up massively and comprehensively in the lav at your shop – I had to hack my way through the audience; you can't have missed that.'

'No, well, you went to the loo at one point, yes. I didn't know you were feeling unwell.'

'Didn't know . . . But, wait a minute, I went to sleep during the reading. Didn't I do that?'

'Did you? Can't have been for more than a second or two. I certainly didn't notice.'

'Or that I was shitfaced?'

'Not at all. You must hold your drink pretty well, that's all I can say.'

A miracle. It's a miracle. And as Alan's assurances mount up, so the skull-clamps case and the black bile in my gut begins to dissolve. *Not guilty.* But wait a moment – the party.

'Alan, when we got back to your place . . . I had a good time . . . did I?'

'Seemed to enjoy yourself. I remember you danced a bit. Well, we all did.'

'And then –?'

'Then . . . nothing. Went to bed, I expect.'

He pays for breakfast, walks me to the Green Line station and waves me off. I wave back. I am beginning to formulate the notion that drunks look better, behave better, *act* better than they sometimes think. I survive the bus-ride and get home where – sure – I throw up, but it's little more than a hiccough-and-plop.

A week later and I'm having a drink at the Pillars of Hercules with Ian Hamilton. We're catching up. He asks me to review a volume of poetry. I say I hate that poet's work. He says, Exactly. I say, *en passant*, that I gave a reading at Alan Hancox's bookshop last week. He says, 'I know.' His eyebrow lifts a fraction; and there's that lopsided smile. Suddenly, the head-clamps are back, and the black bile.

I say, 'Go on.'

'I was on the phone to Alan and he mentioned you'd been up there.'

'What did he say?'

'In so many words?' Ian chuckles. He becomes Alan Hancox on the phone:

It was fantastic! David Harsent was totally rat-arsed! He stag-gered about talking drivel, he left the restaurant without paying his share, he passed out and snored through most of the reading, he threw up at top-decibels in the shop loo, he signed his books inde-cipherably, he told people repeatedly to fuck off, he danced round my living room like a wallaby on amphetamines, he propositioned every woman in the place, he . . .

'The drowning man is not troubled by rain.' Persian proverb

Carl Hiaasen

Any book event that begins with a near-death experience should be abandoned at once. I learned this lesson the hard way several years ago, when I inexplicably agreed to do a reading at a bookstore in a small town in Arkansas. Getting there required flying first to Memphis on a small, propeller-driven commuter aircraft, not ideally engineered for breaching heavy, low-altitude thunderstorms. The jolting turbulence yanked the earphones of my Sony Walkman off my head, just as a mountainous woman next to me began singing Bible hymns at the top of her lungs. The trip was so dreadful that the pilot insisted on apologizing to each of us personally after our very rough, but welcomed, landing.

Instead of bolting straight to the nearest bar, I idiotically climbed in a rental car for the long rainy drive to the bookstore. That leg of the journey also brought adventure as a tractor-trailer rig jack-knifed a mile or so ahead of me, rolled over and effectively blocked the interstate highway in both directions. At this point a sane person would have understood that

God was trying to send a message; I, however, was on a mission to sell books. Blithely I steered at high speed off the pavement, dodging the mangled truck and motoring onward through the rotten weather.

Here I must backtrack to recall an important clue that I had foolishly overlooked. Months earlier, after agreeing to add the Arkansas event to my book tour, I had been asked in all earnestness if I wanted to be a 'celebrity' judge in the town's famous chili cook-off, which by lucky coincidence would be taking place on the same day of my arrival, in the same shopping strip where the bookstore was located. I had demurred, citing phantom gastroenterological disorders. In retrospect, I should have recognized the chili-tasting invitation as the dark omen it was, and cancelled the gig immediately.

When I finally found the bookstore, I noticed that it was as quiet as a morgue, and as empty of life. I chose to attribute this to the torrential downpour and prevailing tornado warnings, and not to any lack of enthusiasm for my novels. The proprietress of the store, a lovely and gracious woman, assured me that hordes of loyal readers would descend at the first break in the weather.

I passed the time – and time passes slowly in Arkansas, I assure you – chatting with the store clerks, one of whom let it slip that I was competing that afternoon not only with the chili-cooking contest but also with the annual college football game between the University of Arkansas Razorbacks and, I believe, the University of Oklahoma Sooners. A casual stroll through the shopping plaza confirmed the dismal fact; everyone seemed to have a bowl of chili and a portable radio tuned to football. A reporter for the local AM station was supposed to interview me during half-time, but evidently he'd gotten so swept up in the game that he forgot.

So I trudged back to the bookstore and waited patiently for someone, anyone, to walk through the front door. Eventually the owner said I might as well take advantage of the 'lull' and sign one of the wooden folding chairs that she had set up for the anticipated throngs. Over the years I'd autographed posters, photos, bumper stickers, even a young woman's chest, but never had I been asked to put my signature on a piece of cheap patio furniture. The owner explained that it was a popular tradition at her store, and indeed led me to a stack of chairs autographed by visiting authors, the most notable of whom was John Grisham. Naturally I whipped out my Sharpie and signed one with a flourish.

Eventually the rain tapered off, but nobody ever showed up to hear me read. So I didn't; I sat. As the final excruciating minutes ticked down, I personalized a copy of my novel for each of the store clerks (who would have rather gone that day to the football game), and also for one or two of the store owner's relatives (who were kind enough to stop by and pretend to be customers).

As my freshly autographed chair was unceremoniously folded away with the others, the store owner said she felt terrible about the 'low turnout', and professed to be mystified. I declined with heroic politesse when she offered a hot cup of homemade chili for my journey back to the Memphis airport.

'If you have any shame, forbear to pluck the beard of a dead lion.'
Martial, *Epigrams*

Geoff Dyer

Dear Robin,
I hear that you are publishing an anthology of pieces on the theme of literary mortification. Well, I have to say that I was very disappointed – mortified actually – not to be asked, especially when I heard the names of some of the writers you *did* ask (most of them friends of yours, I imagine, or people you publish). Some people have short memories, evidently. No doubt you have forgotten that I once specifically asked my agent to offer the manuscript of one of my novels to you even though she wanted to send it to a more established 'literary' imprint (I think you were at Cape at the time). Anyway, you have come a long way since then and have probably forgotten this and, frankly, I'd forgotten all about it too until I heard of this anthology and decided I'd drop you a note since it has been a long time since we were in touch. I think the last time was when you were editing *Firebird* at Penguin and I wrote a quite hostile review of it in the *Literary Review*. Surely that doesn't still rankle with you, does it? Some people have long

memories, evidently. Personally, I'd completely forgotten about that too and I'm surprised you haven't. 'Get a life!' as Helen Simpson (I suppose *she*'s in it) would say.

Actually, it occurs to me that you might be harbouring a more recent grudge. A couple of years ago I wrote quite a vicious review of a book you published: Thomas Lynch's *The Undertaking*. Obviously it is galling – one might even say *mortifying* in this instance! – when your authors are reviewed unfavourably but you have to respect the critical integrity of the reviewer's judgement, especially since I did not know you were the publisher at the time and, obviously, would not have written what I did if I *had* known.

Anyway, to get back to your latest project. I can imagine what these tales of woe are like without even reading them. Let me guess . . . Will Self on how he did an event with Irvine Welsh and the line for people wanting copies of *Trainspotting* went right round the world and the queue of people who were there for him only went twice round the block. Well, I've taken a lot of drugs too but some of us choose not to write about it the whole time. The older I get, in fact, the less patience I have with writers who are narcissistically preoccupied with themselves and their own experience.

So yes, I've got a pretty good idea of what these hard luck stories are like and I have to say my heart is breaking. Spare me. Well, obviously you have spared me by not asking me to write anything and, as it happens, I am far too busy anyway. One thing you can be sure about: if I ever edit an anthology of great literary triumphs I won't be asking you to contribute. In fact I won't be asking *anyone* to contribute. That book will only have one contributor and it'll be *me*.

Having said that, if you decide that the anthology would benefit from some *serious* writing do get into touch with me directly (I don't have an agent any more). I doubt if I would have the time to do something but it might be worth giving me a call on the off-chance if the book has not gone to press yet.

Yours
Geoff Dyer

PS: I could turn it around quite quickly and would not require a fee.

'He hears
On all sides, from innumerable tongues
A dismal universal hiss, the sound
Of public scorn.'
Milton, *Paradise Lost*

Nicola Barker

I had a bad night in Wales. I was reading from my novel *Wide Open*. The gist of my presentation was that this was a novel which it was impossible to do a reading from. I was wedged between Alan Hollinghurst and Rupert Thomson. I ended up reminiscing – and at some length – about how my boyfriend once suffered from a series of spectacular nosebleeds while we were on holiday in Madrid, and how I could never really feel sympathetically inclined towards tapas after that.

Later we were led to an adjacent tent where we were to do a signing. Somewhere close by – in a much bigger venue – Terry Pratchett had just completed a public appearance. The signing tent was soon packed with Pratchett fans. I was standing behind a table, waiting (in vain) for somebody to buy a book. At this point I was approached by an angry-looking woman holding Pratchett's latest and waving a ten-pound note. She shoved the book at me.

'I'm sorry,' I whispered apologetically (five years' experience as a bakery cashier, all coming to nothing), 'but I don't actually work here. I'm one of the authors.'

'I don't give a damn who you are,' she hissed, 'just take the fucking money.'

Afterwards, on my long walk home to a rather isolated cottage where several of the authors were staying, I saw two genial-looking teenagers strolling, hand-in-hand, along the empty country road towards me. I was carrying a box of champagne (the payment for the reading, and a drink which makes me violently ill), and I was struggling.

It took several minutes for us to draw adjacent. As they passed by, the boy-teen said, 'You're Nicola Barker, aren't you?' I stopped, panting slightly; 'Yes, I am.'

'We just went to see you reading,' he said.

'Oh, right,' I puffed. 'Did you enjoy it?'

No answer.

'We took your book *Reversed Forecast* on holiday with us last year,' the girl-teen eventually continued, 'and I was so irritated by it that I forced him to read it.'

He nodded. 'Neither of us understood the ending. We were so infuriated by the whole experience that we travelled all the way down here tonight, in hope of some kind of clarification . . .' He paused, glancing down witheringly at my box of champagne. 'But I'm afraid we didn't get any.'

'A guest sees more in an hour than the host in a year.'
Polish proverb

Bernard MacLaverty

Sometimes organizations are genuinely broke and you find
yourself agreeing to eat with the organizer's in-laws.

We – the organizer and myself along with a couple of local
writers – arrived at the in-laws' apartment in good time. The
organizer pressed the bell and this started a cacophonous barking. Enough for two dogs. Then a female voice screamed 'Stop
it – Jules. Jim, stop it this minute.'

We heard scrabbling at the lock and were unsure if it was
the dogs or the hostess trying to open the door. The door
opened a fraction. And the barking got louder.

A small woman peered out. But before she could do anything one of the dogs squirmed between her legs and dashed
about the marble landing fit to burst.

It was a boxer – caramel-coloured with a black savage face.
Another boxer followed before the woman could get her legs
closed. The dogs flung themselves at the visitors' genitals but
sheered off at the last moment. They continued to attack while
the hostess continued to shout at them. 'Jules – Jim – stop it

this minute.' They barked loudly and continuously, racing to and fro, interfering with every movement the guests made. I tried to move slowly and deliberately so's not to startle or anger the dogs any more than was necessary. I'm terrified of dogs. I don't remember it but I'm told when I was a baby in a pram I was bitten on the head by a next-door dog called Trixie – so somewhere in my subconscious I'm shit scared.

A boxer is sitting back on his haunches in front of me barking to burst ear-drums and baring his teeth and I am trying to be pleasant to the hostess. The other dog is somewhere behind me. The light from the hallway shows that in their excitement the dogs have been pissing all over the place – including my shoes and trousers. 'Look what you're doing – Jules, Jim, stop right now,' she yells. The dogs seem demented – squirting piss left, right and centre as they race around the landing and hallway, their claws scraping. 'How dare you! Get up to your bed. Get inside this minute.' I'm trying to air-kiss the hostess as she screams and goes through great bouts of eye-rolling. 'Delighted to meet you,' I say and she nods. The next guest in line attempts to embrace her but she bends down and catches either Jules or Jim by the studded collar and flings him bodily down the hallway. They race out of sight into another room. 'How dare you! This happens every time. Jim, Jules, I'll not warn you again.' They are in the distance for a moment or two.

The hostess straightens up and completes greeting the other guests. What a total nonsense all this is. This scene must happen every time the door-bell rings. These people invited us. We came on time. Why weren't these hounds put somewhere else? Our hostess says, 'They're perfectly harmless – they wouldn't touch you – they're just a bit excited by strangers.' So it's the guests who are causing the problem. They're the ones to blame. If they weren't here the dogs would be sleeping. Everyone starts taking off their coats and still the barking goes on. The dogs come racing out of a distant room and launch another attack. They must be like real boxers and fight three-minute rounds. Bounding and yapping. Pissing and scraping. 'Stop it! Jules! Jim!' They are incredibly ugly creatures with their faces of black wrinkled skin and white bared teeth. I freeze when one lunges. Very slowly and deliberately, in as non-threatening a gesture as I can muster, I hand my coat over to the hostess.

Eventually everyone gets into the living room and sits down, keeping very still. The dogs leap up on the furniture and their owners create more noise than the dogs. 'Get down. Jules! Jim! On the floor.'

'Don't you dare!' Both dogs jump up onto the sofa beside me. They give me an eyeful of their backsides before I can look away. Boxers have whorls, little whirlpools of hair on either side of their black leathery asshole. People don't want to dwell on that kind of detail just before they eat but when it's been there, close-up, the image can't be erased.

The hostess gets everyone to their feet and shepherds them into a dining room which looks out on a balcony. It seems she and her husband ate earlier for health reasons. They will come to the table but they will not eat. They are old and not at all healthy, despite having eaten earlier. Things can be heard in their chests. He is overweight and his lips have a disturbing bluish tinge. The curve of his belly is emphasized by one of those Fair-Isle golf sweaters. Even they realize that the dogs should be controlled in some way and the hostess puts them out onto the balcony. The creatures proceed to whine and scratch loudly against the balcony doors. They also snort and blow beneath them.

Dishes are brought to the table by the hostess. Everyone eats as the mother and father-in-law smoke one cigarette after another. The soup tastes of something indefinable. Dog piss, maybe. It is not bad, but faint – a distant tinge of raven fat or bat droppings – like something never tasted before and not altogether appetizing. The dogs on the balcony are creating such a din of scratching and whingeing that one of the guests suggests letting them in. It would be quieter. The hostess gets up and opens the door. The dogs rush past her with delight. They run in and out, beneath the table, under our chairs. As they slaver and slabber, strings of white mucus hang from their jowls. I keep my knees together to prevent the dogs getting in there for a good sniff at my crotch. That stuff would look bad on your trousers. Every so often throughout the meal, my hand strays down and I immediately sense a wet engulfment. A dog's nose is like a dish of cold snails.

After the soup comes the main course. The hostess serves a dish of peas and ham. It has been cooked in the same raven fat or bat droppings which was used to such effect in the soup. The ham is maroon to black, thickly stratified with white. There is a not-fully-poached egg in the middle of the peas. I cut the egg and watch the yolk leak out into the green sur-roundings. Then the old man has a coughing fit. It sounds like he's tumbling gravel deep in his chest or regurgitating lightly poached eggs. When it's over and he is sufficiently recovered he lights another cigarette. There is a distinct splashing sound. Jules is taking a piss on the tiles of the hallway. The door-bell rings and the dogs go apeshit again.

I put down my fork and glance down at my watch. There are several hours to go. The local red wine is excellent and seems the only refuge. I get tore in.

'Of all the thirty-six alternatives, running away is best.'
Chinese proverb

Simon Armitage

Literature offers endless opportunities for embarrassment and humiliation because it operates at that boundary where private thought meets its public response. Live literary events are the front-line, the human interface between writing and reading. Sometimes the two elements mix, sometimes they curdle, and sometimes they stand like oil and water, resolute and opposed. I give readings at least a hundred times each year. No single incident amounts to much more than an anecdote, but when taken as a whole . . .

I am met off the train by an extremely nervous woman in a hire-car who is generating a thermo-nuclear amount of heat and cannot locate the de-mist function on the console. In a cloud of condensation we drive to a local café where she restricts my choice of meal according to her authorized budget. I have forgotten to bring any books. I visit the local bookshop to purchase a copy of my *Selected Poems* and am recognized by the man at the till. He says nothing, but his expression is one of pathos.

The venue is a Portakabin in a car-park. The p.a. system is a Fisher-Price press'n' play karaoke machine. I am introduced as, 'The name on everyone's lips: Simon Armriding'. A well-intentioned youth doing voluntary work for the aurally challenged (of which there is none in the audience) has offered to 'sign'. He stands to my left all evening, giving what is a passable impersonation of Ian Curtis dancing to 'She's Lost Control Again' and eventually passes out. Five minutes before the interval, a nice lady from the WI goes into the kitchenette at the back to begin tea-making operations. My final poem of the half is accompanied by the organ-like hum of a wall-mounted water-heater rising slowly towards boiling point. There is no alcohol but how about a cup of Bovril? Following the break, an old man at the front falls asleep and farts during a poem about death/suffering/self pity, etc. Afterwards, there are no books for sale but some kind soul asks me to autograph her copy of *Summoned by Bells*.

My designated driver, the radio-active woman, transports me in her mobile sauna to an Indian restaurant on the high street. She is allergic to curry (for fear of melt-down, presumably) but waits for me in the car while I guzzle a meal of not more than five pounds in value (including drinks) paid for by food voucher. I am staying with old Mr Farter in the suburbs. He has gone home to give the Z-bed an airing and to prepare a selection of his poems for my perusal, the first of which, 'The Mallard', begins, 'Thou, oh monarch of the riverbank'. I 'sleep' fully-clothed on a pube-infested sheet.

Ungraciously and with great stealth I leave the house before dawn and wander through empty, unfamiliar avenues heading vaguely towards the tallest buildings on the skyline. It is three hours before the first train home. I breakfast with winos and junkies in McDonald's. Killing time in the precinct, I find a

copy of one of my early volumes in a dump-bin on the pavement outside the charity shop. The price is ten pence. It is a
signed copy. Under the signature, in my own handwriting,
are the words, 'To mum and dad'.

'Memory is the thing you forget with.' Alexander Chase

Julian Barnes

It was my first literary party, in a London garden. I was in my late twenties, a hand-to-mouth reviewer with no day job. I took a girl I wasn't quite going out with. We ran into a friend of mine. 'This is Chris Reid,' I said. 'What do you do?' she asked. 'I'm a poet,' he replied. She laughed with such forceful scorn that she recoiled back into a flower-bed and spilled half her wine. When Chris had wandered off, I asked why she'd reacted like that. 'You can't say you're a poet if you *just write poems*,' she answered. I felt glad I had never described myself – to anyone, let alone her – as a novelist, even though my desk contained the full draft of a novel.

The party moved on. Someone introduced me to Elizabeth Jane Howard, and then scarpered. She seemed to me formidable: tall, poised, coiffed and gowned, waiting to be diverted out of some grand boredom. As it happened, I had recently reviewed a collection of her short stories, *Mr Wrong*, for the *Oxford Mail*; better still, I had been enthusiastic about them. I mentioned this as unobsequiously as I could; she was neither diverted nor, as far as I could tell, remotely interested. Fair enough. 'I gave you a decent review in a four-book fiction round-up in a provincial newspaper,' or words to that effect, was probably not the conversational key to literary London.

How to engage her? Something more recherché, perhaps. I remembered, in a book-nerdish way, that whereas collections of stories normally list on the reverse of the title page the original places of serial publication, there were no such attributions in *Mr Wrong*. I decided that such silence must have been a deliberate authorial decision. I wondered what her reasons might have been. I asked her about it.

'I didn't know that was the case.'

'Ah.'

'No.'

'So it wasn't deliberate?'

'No.'

The conversation was definitely lacking brio. I doubted she would be interested in my own modest literary breakthrough. A few months previously I had entered a Ghost Story competition organized by *The Times*, had been chosen as one of the dozen winners, and was soon to be rewarded with publication in a hardback anthology by Jonathan Cape! Who were Elizabeth Jane Howard's own publishers!! No, she definitely wouldn't be interested in that.

I gazed rather desperately across the party and saw a tall, windblown figure who could well be Tom Maschler. What a coincidence – the editorial boss of Jonathan Cape.

'Is that by any chance . . . Tom Maschler?'

'Yes, would you like to meet him?' she replied instantly, then marched me across and left me there.

My nerves were by now pretty shot. Still, I wanted to try and impress.

'Hello,' I said, 'I'm one-twelfth of one of your authors.'

He didn't look even faintly amused. I explained ploddingly about *The Times Anthology of Ghost Stories* and its dozen contributors. He asked me my name again. I told him again. He shook his head.

'Sorry, I don't remember names. What was the title of your story?'

I looked at him. He looked back expectantly. I paused. My mind was filled with a terrible blank. What the *fuck* was the title of my story? I knew it, I was sure I knew it. Come on, come on, you've just read the proofs. You've just written your own contributor's note. This is your publisher. You *must* know. It's impossible for you *not* to know.

'I can't remember,' I replied.

So there we were: a publisher who didn't recognize one of his writers' names, and a writer who couldn't remember the title of his own – his only – work. Welcome to the literary life.

And the girl I wasn't quite going out with? Oh, she dumped me soon afterwards.

'It is a hard matter for a man to go down into the valley of Humiliation ... and to catch no slip by the way.'
Bunyan, *Pilgrim's Progress*

Rick Moody

You're lucky to go on tour. You're lucky to meet readers who prize your work and who seem as though they might be honoured to meet you. You're lucky to eat the pretzels in the mini-bar. You're lucky to see cities you have never seen, like Cincinnati and Baltimore. These things are indisputable. Anyone will tell you.

It was my first time, for a novel called *The Ice Storm*. Not a big tour, because it was my first. Six cities. Minneapolis, L.A., San Francisco, Seattle, Boston, DC. Most of the audiences numbered in the single digits. When I called my publicist in NYC, she offered consolations: it was *so* important to *break in new audiences*.

What if my heart broke first?

I managed to survive the first five cities. Then it was time to go to DC. *Our nation's capital.* Back then, my mom didn't live too far from DC. She lived in Virginia. She volunteered to come up to hear me read. This was complicated for a few reasons. My mother had a lot of opinions about my work, not all good. She once reviewed a book by me on Amazon.com and gave me three out of five stars. Then she told me that it was a *positive* review.

I gave my name at the hotel, and the woman at the front desk seemed incredibly impressed. 'Mr Moody, we are honoured to have you here in the hotel!' Or some similarly inflated greeting. I can't imagine who the desk clerk thought I might be. A diplomat from the nation state of Dishevelment. Or a high-ranking functionary from the Association for Arrested Development. Nevertheless, she took the VIP designation on her reservation list to heart, and she ladled on politeness.

Probably I'd stayed in a *suite* as a kid, or visited one. But not by myself. Never had I roamed lonely through the extra living room with the extra fax machine and the extra mini-bar for pilfering, etc. Never had I watched hotel porn on someone else's credit card. This was clearly the beginning of world domination. This was clearly the beginning of Rick Moody, branding opportunity; Rick Moody, LLC.

My mother called from the front desk. She came up. We had tea. How civilized. I could see here in the *suite*, drinking tea with my mother, that my tides were turning.

Later, we headed out for the bookstore where I was to read. The publicist had made clear that this was a *great* DC store. *Great reading series!*

Humiliation is imminent. Let's just skip ahead. It began upon passing through the threshold of the store. 'Mr Moody!' a young woman with glasses said good-naturedly. 'Thanks for coming!' I looked around. Even by the standards of my six-city tour, where double-digit audiences were an accomplishment, things were looking sparse.

The young woman with spectacles herded me toward one

wall, probably in the psychology section. 'There has been a little problem we'd like to tell you about. We're really sorry about it. But there was a–'

'Yes?'

A typo in the schedule! *A typo in the schedule.* A typo!

'The schedule we mailed out shows you as reading last night. I'm so sorry.'

The schedule was empty for the night. So was the store.

'Someone did leave a note for you, though.'

She handed over the note as though it would compensate for the typo in the schedule. 'Dear Rick, so sorry I'm not going to be able to make the reading tonight. I was looking forward to it, but something came up. Hope it goes well. See you soon. Elise.'

Well, I'd *almost* had an audience member. Besides my mom. Who was cowering over in history, pretending that nothing bad was happening.

Then, as if according to miracle, a friend *did* stride into the store. Katya, the art historian from New York. She went to high school with my brother, smoked pot with him, and then became a very successful art critic. At present, she was the only person in the audience who had not expelled me from her uterus.

'We'll wait just a few more minutes for the stragglers,' the girl with the glasses said eagerly. I disappeared into the stacks. Several minutes passed there, and the little bell in the door at the bookstore did not jingle even once. At last, I trudged miserably to the table that served as my podium. The little table before the entirely empty constellation of chairs, wherein Katya and my mother sat, as apart from one another as they could sit. No, wait! Now there was a gentleman edging into the audience. A homeless guy? Maybe. He'd definitely never been to a reading before, nor since.

Here I was in *our nation's capital*, at this, the dawn of my career, and I was reading, as briefly as possible, to my mother, to a woman who had smoked pot with my brother in high school, and to a guy persuaded to sit through the reading for 10% off any purchase. My mother wore a frozen smile throughout. The truth was plain to see. My career as a fiction writer was launched! And it was founded upon neglect, disappointment, misunderstanding, familial resentment, and typos.

'Disease makes men more physical, it leaves them nothing but body.' Thomas Mann

Paul Farley

Several years ago I was in India doing some work for the British Council, and I'd been enjoying the visit until, towards the end, I was pole-axed with a stomach upset. The flight back to Heathrow set the tenor for the next few weeks: panic in public or confined spaces, long spells hunched on a toilet. My GP in Brighton thought it was 'Delhi belly', and wouldn't respond to antibiotics, so didn't bother prescribing any (I found out, over a year later when my notes had been trans-ferred up to the Lake District, that I'd had campylobacter with e-coli cysts). I had a few engagements coming up, one of which involved a reading: what to do? For some reason – and I'm at a loss now to account for this – I decided to go ahead. It'd be OK. I'd shut myself down with Imodium. I couldn't cancel: they'd sent out flyers and everything.

Under normal circumstances, it would have been the most straightforward of gigs, but the state of my bowels knocked everything out of whack. On the train it was easier to stay locked in the toilet for the journey. The Imodium wasn't really kicking in. I was supposed to take a taxi from the station to the venue, but I didn't fancy being sat in a cab in an 'historic city' I didn't really know, stuck in traffic, a driver trying to chat to me. So I walked it, stopping off at McDonald's, British Home Stores, Waterstone's, Boots and a pub along the way: I still remember the place as a series of disabled toilets, and can recall the graffiti I sat staring at for minutes on end better than its architecture. What did Edward Hopper say about our impressions when entering or leaving a city? But I shouldn't try to raise the tone.

I rolled up in a pretty undignified state, but nobody seemed to notice when I was met, and I'd come this far, etc. The reading was in an arts centre, and about thirty people had shown up I was told. I always smile to myself when people rue the state of poetry in these islands, with its phoney populism and hype, its pandering to audiences. What events had they been going to? The reality – at least the one I've experienced repeatedly – is an edge-of-town arts centre, a small audience listening carefully, a few books sold, a fumbling for receipts. I'd never been so aware of the discrepancy, waiting to go on that evening, a flop sweat staining through my jacket. I can't recall how much scratch I was doing it for.

If it wasn't money that got me out of my sickbed, then it must have been stupidity. Sitting there, anxiety began to take hold. I've been mildly nervous before giving readings, but this was of a new, suffocating order I'd never experienced before (or since, I'm happy to say). I wondered whether the microphone would pick up the squawks and whines my insides were making. The organizer of the event was introducing me, and she was giving it the full welly. I was a rising star, I was one of the most talented voices to have emerged in recent years, I was hip, I was full of pop-cultural references, I was a crackling performer, I was laddish, and I stepped up to the stage wearing a broad, confident grin and, unbeknownst to my audience, a press-on towel.

'Ignorance and incuriosity are two very soft pillows.'
French proverb

Edna O'Brien

In the heady Sixties, I was not long in London when I had been mysteriously invited to a dinner party, somewhere in Belgravia. I was seated next to Groucho Marx, whom I can safely say was one of the most reserved and taciturn people I have ever met. Eventually and in answer to some garbled compliment of mine, he asked me what I did. I confessed to being a writer. He recognized that I was Irish and had a moment of rumination with himself, then called across to his wife, who was seated at another table, to ask the name of the young Irish woman who wrote hilariously about convent life and whom they both so admired. I waited, already basking in the ensuing compliment, but as the fates would have it, the writer they admired was Bridget Brophy.

That glorified term 'book tour'. It was a department store in Birmingham, a busy Saturday with shoppers coming and going and myself at a table with piles of my novel *Johnny I Hardly Knew You* stacked around me. Mothers, with small children, irate children, restless children, passed by without giving me a second look. No one stopped to buy a book, or even glance. News of this mounting failure must have reached someone in an upper office because presently it was announced on the tannoy that I would be happy to sign copies of my novel, just hot off the press. I waited and looked at people, embarrassed. My pleas were not returned, nor were my prayers. When the hour at last had expired, I got up, withdrew into my coat as into a shell and thanked a young assistant who said, 'Got to laugh, love, haven't you.' At the main door I was accosted by a fellow countryman – inebriated – who enquired if I was me and then with familiar spunk said 'Would you ever loan us a fiver.' I am quite proud of my reply – 'I'll give it to you because it's not likely that I'll be back here again.'

I am attending a performance of my play *Virginia* at the Haymarket Theatre and I am alone. Just before the curtain of the first act, there was a somewhat spry, erotically charged scene between Virginia Woolf and Vita Sackville-West, played with verve by Maggie Smith and Patricia Connolly. As the lights came up, the two women who were behind me and who had been muttering throughout, yielded to a state of high dudgeon and moral indignation. I had got it wrong. 'She's got it quite wrong, Vita Sackville-West was a married woman with children and here we are being told that she is a lesbian, a lesbian,' one of them said. Her companion shook her head in exemplary disgust and then in imperious tone delivered her coup – 'But of course she's got it wrong darling, Edna O'Brien writes for servants, everyone knows that.' They received the full brunt of my glacial stare and scurried off.

'Radio and television . . . have succeeded in lifting the manufacture of banality out of the sphere of handicraft and placed it in that of a major industry.' Nathalie Sarraute

Andrew O'Hagan

Maybe I'm just being excessively Catholic, but I've long suspected there might be a certain, defiant, limited pleasure to be had in the pain of humiliation. After all, embarrassment reminds us as much of our abundant needs as our abject failings, and a writer might do well to listen carefully to the drama of his own requirements. In the true black night of humiliation, in the bloodletting hours, a writer becomes most fully and most properly himself. We might venture to call it the Writer's Life: the only success you can count on is success on the page; the rest – golden whispers from the F. Scott Fitzgerald handbook of instant triumph – are nothing more than throat-clearing exercises in preparation for the three-act opera of mortification that must follow.

Aged twenty-six, with an acre of smiles and hopes, I was very happy to find myself on my first American book tour. The weather was fine, the *New York Times* liked my book, I had a new suit, and I went from city to city in a mild swoon of short drinks and long evenings, feeling certain the writer's game was my kind of fun. Everywhere I went, it seemed, there was someone new stepping forward with a kind proposal: write for the *New Yorker*, come on the *Studs Terkel Show*, travel to Butte, Montana, marry my daughter; the days grew long with sustainable pleasures, and I understood it would only be a matter of time before I was asked to give the State of the Union Address. Then my plane and my self-satisfaction broke through the clouds to land in Chicago.

Now, Chicago is a friendly town. There are plenty of college kids and small magazines: they liked the book, and, if you were happily stupid, as I was, you might have allowed yourself to imagine that their enthusiasm described a general mood, that the whole of America indeed was turgid that day with love and recognition for the author of *The Missing* – a non-fictional meditation on the subject of missing persons. At that early stage I was not familiar with the concept of the 'quiet news day', therefore, when a producer from *Good Morning Chicago* rang to invite me on, I could only imagine they too were gasping for a bit of the O'Hagan goodness.

The make-up room was quiet at eight a.m. Around the wall they had framed photographs of American comics – Phyllis Diller, I remember, and Sid Caesar, caught laughing in that particular limelight-drunk way I'd been rehearsing since New Jersey – and so I sat in the chair with a perfect sense of belonging as the girl got to work with her orange sponge. A blonde woman was sitting in the next chair along and we caught one another's eye. She was smiling at me, and something in her experienced face seemed to draw all the light from the lightbulbs surrounding the large mirror. 'Do you mind if I say something to you?' she asked.

'No bother,' I said.

'Well. You look like you've got a whole lot of God in you,'

she said, her elastic smile seeming quickly to lunge across her cheek to land in a snarl.

'God?' I said. 'Well, it's been a good week, but . . .'

'Definitely,' she said. 'Definitely God. Like Godliness.'

She put out her hand between the chairs. 'My name's Dana Plato,' she said. 'You probably know me?' (Her voice had that semi-plaintive, questing upward swing at the end of sentences, the one Americans deploy so effectively, seeming hurt and demanding at the same time.) 'I used to be in a big TV show called *Diff'rent Strokes*. It was really huge.'

She was speaking to me now in the mirror.

'There was a lot of bad luck on the show,' she said. 'Everybody on the show, well . . . all of us, we had bad luck.'

'Really?' I said. But I knew fine well who she was. *Diff'rent Strokes* was a feature of my Scottish youth, famous for Gary Coleman, the bizarrely small black guy with the grin and the catchphrase – 'What you talk'n' about?' – and Dana Plato played the wise-cracking girl in his adoptive family. I even knew about the 'bad luck': it had been a tabloid story for years, 'The Curse of *Diff'rent Strokes*', but I stared at her in the mirror as my face became more orange and her eyes got glittery with memory.

'I got busted for armed robbery. It was a video store in Vegas,' she said. 'It was money, you know? And the other guys on the show . . . oh, there was guns and more drugs, the whole deal.'

'God,' I said.

'Absolutely,' she said. 'I got out of all that when I became a Christian, and I went to rehab, and now I'm here in Chicago to star in a wonderful show called *Hollywood's Greatest Moments*.'

I had to consider this for a second. Dana Plato was sitting next to me. She was wired. She was going on the show. With her blonde hair, her video store saga, her Godliness, the new production opening tonight – Jesus Christ almighty! How was any poor bugger supposed to compete?

'She says you're a *wrider*,' said Dana.

'Yes,' I said.

'I love *wriders*. You're a famous *wrider*, good heavens.'

'No. Not at all,' I said. 'I've just started . . .'

'Gee,' she said. 'A famous *wrider*. And we're on the same show. You must be famous. You're being cute. They don't usually have *wriders* on shows like this.'

Several sorts of panic entered my soul at once. Some of those panics are the sort that might cause you to feel pity for me, but others were only shaming, and reveal a native understanding of the machinations of showbusiness self-interest the likes of which might serve to make Diana Ross look like Miss Congeniality. I took a deep breath and asked the most selfish question of my career. 'On the show: am I following you?'

'Yes. I think so,' said Dana.

My heart almost erupted in the lower depths. I could just imagine it out there: first up, Mrs Popular-70s-TV-Show-Insider-Gossip-Rags-to-Riches-Riches-to-Rags-to-Riches-Motherfuck-ing-Video-Store-Robbing-Rehab-Attending-God-Discovering-and-Now-Topping-the-Bill-in-Hollywood's-Greatest-Moments-Goddam-Arse-Shattering-Showbusiness-Miracle-Survival-Ex-travaganza-Big-it-Up-to-the-High-Fucken-Heavens-for-Miss-Dana Plato!, thereafter to be immediately followed onstage by Young Mr Who-the-Fuck-is-He-With-His-Motherfucking-Nonentity-Book-and-Giant-British-Forehead-Dishing-Out-All-Sorts-of-Boring-and-Depressing-Crap-About-Missing-People-in-His-Weird-Accent. Jesus Christ! It was going to be a blood-bath. It was going to be the massacre at Glencoe. Dana Plato was showbiz King Kong and I was scantily-clad Fay Wray writhing in her massive, pounding, hairy palm.

I asked her again.

'Is that right? They have ME following YOU?'

'Yeh. I love your accent. You're cute.'

Somewhere in the universe, the applause for Dana Plato is still resounding and travelling, and the flow of love from that Chicago audience is still passing star formations that are yet to be observed by the strongest telescopes on earth. To say they loved Dana Plato will not do: they wanted Dana Plato for ever, they wanted the story of Dana Plato to go on and on, and for the message of Dana to sing out and fill all the terrible voids in our lives. They wanted Dana to never stop talking, never stop being, and for every home in America to keep an eternal light shining on their porches for the wise and suffering existence of Dana Plato.

Then I came on. The show was live. The studio set – like all those studio sets in America – looked like a terrifying screech of blue optimism under the yellow lights, and the studio audience was invisible as I took my place on the sofa. The two 'anchors' in front of me were the very soul of mild-mannered derision: attentive to nothing but their earpieces, they bent lovingly into the visiting powder brush – it was the ad break – and continued praising the departed Dana.

'You bet. Just terrific. Super-terrific. You bet.'

My new suit felt old. I felt old. My hair felt old and my limbs felt heavy and my shiny-covered new book seemed dead on the table between us. I looked at the two presenters and made a swift and expensive mental note: they had that look, the anchors, that look that male American television presenters often have, that android appearance, sprayed-in, perma-tanned, so handsome they're ugly. 'Yeah,' I heard one of them say to the gallery. 'Keeping it short.'

The adverts were over. I could hear someone count down across the dark studio floor. 'Okay!'

'Welcome back. You're watching *Good Morning Chicago*. Wasn't Dana Plato just terrific? Well, let's move on. Maybe you're watching with your family this morning. We all have families, and our next guest, Andrew O'Hagan, is from Scotland. He is a writer, and he's just produced a book about his grandfather.'

All the cables on the studio floor, raised up like snakes by the oily charm of the android, seemed to sway before me and hiss. I saw the whole sorry affair in a moment of surreal clarity amidst the piercing yellow of the studio: I had travelled far from home and got pissed on America; I had got myself drunk on small beer and fast cheer and now I was facing the terrible upchuck of a deluded fortnight. They knew and they loved Dana Plato, superstar, super-being, and now, here I was, Andrew O'Hagan from Scotland, Nonentity of the Century, being interviewed vigorously about a book that I HADN'T WRITTEN!

The point about humiliation, of course, is that it attracts more humiliation to itself. As a general rule, when someone tries to interview you about someone else's book on live television, you don't trust to your own character, you don't put him down, you don't express surprise at his stupidity and walk off – no, you don't do any of those things. You sit up straight, you smile in a friendly way, you look at the dumb fucker with an earnestness that not only pays tribute to his but actually outstrips his, and you say something like the following:

'Well, good morning, Chuck. It's interesting you should ask about grandfathers and families because as you said everybody has one and they're very important. I never actually knew my grandfathers myself, but I know a lot of your viewers will understand the value of community, which is one of the things I set out to tackle in my book *The Missing*.'

'Right,' said Chuck, 'that's interesting.'

Just so's you understand: when an American TV anchor says something like 'that's interesting', it's code for 'can we cut this weird fucker out before he makes us DIE OF BOREDOM?' This is the central rule of the American talk show: it's a stupidity contest, and, no matter what else, you must let the host win.

'But we all love our grandparents,' said Chuck. 'It's a very American thing to love your grandparents. Is that not right?'

'Indeed,' I said. 'Where would we be . . .'

'That's a crazy accent you've got there.'

'I'm from Glasgow, it's . . .'

'Yeah, weird. Now listen, Mr O'Haygone. We don't have much time. Is there some change taking place in the family?'

For a nanosecond I forgot the rules. 'Well, actually. My book is really about missing persons . . .'

'Exactly. There's something missing in the way families relate nowadays. Is that what you're saying?'

'Well, when I was growing up some children went missing and I suppose I always wanted to enter into their story. I thought it would offer a picture of ordinary lives, and I thought I might try to follow the pattern of stories like that, and maybe describe a social atmosphere in the Britain of today.'

'Gee,' said Chuck's sidekick, 'that's some heavy stuff. And have things kinda changed since your grandfather's day?'

'Well, I expect so, and actually, part of my search . . .'

Of all the people who had ever existed in the world, Chuck wanted me to die the most. He wanted me off his fucking show. He wanted Dana Plato back on and he wanted Depressing No Good Bastard from Scotland off his sofa. He wanted it now. He wanted it, like, yesterday. Coolly, with his unreal hair, he peered into the centre of my nonentityhood, and asked his last question.

'Do you have any advice for the mothers of America?'

I already knew my humiliation was complete. I already knew I was lost, so why didn't I seize the chance to be myself? Why didn't I grab him by the lapels in front of his simpering, baby-headed audience of thickos, and say something large, something true and momentous and deserving? Because I'm a coward, that's why, and that's the thing about mortification – it's fed by cowardice. So, when he asked me, a man with no girlfriend and no children, what advice I had for the mothers of America, my true instinct passed like a high-flying flamingo over the jungle-canopy of my sudden humiliation, and I glimpsed it for a second, and thought: Tell him, my advice to the mothers of America is not to stick a wet finger into a live electricity socket, but this coloured bird was gone as soon as it appeared, and I took a breath.

'Not to be too anxious,' I said. 'When it comes to community, and changes in protection for children and families, it's easy to become overwhelmed with the new anxieties. My advice to mothers would be to avoid that if they can.'

'Good advice from this young author out of Scotland. He's been talking about his book about his grandfather and families. Thanks for coming in.'

It was a small round of applause, but it fell like rain, and I walked through the studio and passed faces without words, and before long I was in the limousine, my orange face at the window, and we drove through Chicago, the driver oblivious to the world of authorly humiliations, and me in the back, dreaming of my brand-new life in an igloo somewhere north of Greenland.

'Everyone in a crowd has the power to throw dirt: nine out of ten have the inclination.' William Hazlitt, *On Reading Old Books*

Deborah Moggach

Writers can only moan to each other about all this, really: the humiliating reading to an audience of two, the book-signing where nobody turns up, the talk where the only question is 'Where did you buy your nail varnish?' (I nicked it from my daughter, since you ask). Nobody is really going to care, are they, if we sit alone and unloved beside our pile of books, approached only once in the two hours and that by a woman who is trying to flog us her self-published book on recovering from breast cancer? Or that we wait, alone in the darkness, on the deserted platform at Newark station, the only reading matter a VIOLENT ASSAULT: WITNESSES WANTED sign swinging in the wind, until we realize we've missed the last train home.

There is, however, a certain existential quality to some of these experiences which others can surely share. Humiliation, though one of a writer's specialities, is not an entirely unknown sensation to everybody else. We do expose ourselves, of course, by offering up our work to the world's critical stare, or, worse, its indifference. It's what we sign up for: that people give up their money and their precious time to read about characters who have never existed. And there's a price to be paid for this chutzpah.

I remember a corporate event in Bridlington, where book-shop staff were supposedly wooed by a dinner of scotch eggs and coleslaw into ordering a lot of our books. One of them was a Waterstone's assistant, a stubbly bloke with an earring and a patronizing, 'I only read Don DeLillo' look about him. He was also very drunk. Swaying up to me, he said, 'You write romantic fiction, don't you.' 'No,' I replied. 'Yes you do.' 'Have you read anything of mine?' 'No,' he slurred, 'but I can tell.' 'How?' I asked. 'Because you're an ageing woman wear-ing a leopard-skin top.' To this I replied, with more dignity than he deserved: 'That might make me a romantic, but it doesn't mean I write it.'

'Nationwide Publicity Tour' usually means a couple of sign-ing sessions and two minutes on BBC Radio Humberside. Never is the gulf between promise and reality wider than during an author's publicity tour, at least in my experience. One occasion I remember, almost with fondness, was a pro-motion in a shopping centre in Maidenhead on a rainy Tues-day afternoon. The deal was that if a customer bought a copy of my novel (paperback), they also got a free box of Crabtree and Evelyn freesia soap and a glass of wine. In other words, they were practically being paid to take a book away. Even with these inducements, however, an hour passed and not one single person stopped. 'Oh dear,' said the manageress, 'I don't know what's the matter, it's so embarrassing. We had that Rolf Harris last week and his queue was an hour and a half long.' For some reason she thought that this would make me feel better. Finally, after another half-hour a woman with

Downs Syndrome approached me and asked, 'Do you sell tights?' I directed her to the nearby Dorothy Perkins and off she went. Nobody else came, so I went home.

Often one travels long distances to do a reading. Getting food out of anybody, once one arrives, is always a problem. Drink is even trickier. I remember travelling to the Folkestone Literary Festival, a modest affair in the front room of a defunct seafront hotel, and being offered a small dish of dry-roasted peanuts, to be shared between three authors. We had left London in mid-afternoon and wouldn't get back until midnight but our hostess obviously believed that writers, like Citroën 2CVs, run on very little fuel. Also on very little money, as we were all told, separately, 'Thank you for waiving your usual fee.' (It's a well-known fact that writers are expected to turn up for nothing; try telling that to your plumber.)

Then there was the library in the Midlands where I was booked to do a reading. However far you've travelled to a library you'll be lucky to get a mug of Nescafé, but this one phoned me to ask if I'd like something to eat and drink while I was there. A sandwich and glass of wine would be lovely, I replied. A few days later the phone rang again. 'We've been looking at your photo,' they said, 'and trying to decide if you were a vegetarian.' 'What did you decide?' I asked. 'That you weren't.' I took this as a compliment. They said: 'So we thought we'd buy you a Marks and Spencer salmon sandwich, if that's all right.' 'Lovely,' I replied. Two weeks later I took the train there, to be greeted by the librarians, the sandwich and a lot of fluster. 'We've got you the bottle of wine,' they said, 'but we can't find a corkscrew.' A great deal of scrabbling around followed. 'Have you seen one, Maggie?' 'Didn't Bob have one once?' 'A corkscrew? I don't think so.' 'There must be one somewhere . . .' Cupboards were ransacked. 'Really, I don't mind . . .' I said. 'Please don't bother.' 'No, we've started now and we're going to find it!' they replied. I stood there, feeling like a pervert whose very special needs were going to be satisfied, by hook or by crook, because after all the librarians had promised. Finally the corkscrew was found, the bottle uncorked and some wine solemnly poured into a tea mug. The audience was filing in by now as I stood there, surrounded by librarians, drinking my wine and eating my sandwich. 'I suppose we should have given you a plate,' one of them said.

In Anne Tyler's *The Accidental Tourist* one of the characters runs a factory that makes bottle tops. When asked about it, he replies: 'It's not half as exciting as it sounds.' The same could be said about the publicity tour. What deepens the humiliation is the presence of witnesses – another writer, the bookshop assistants. Their embarrassment and pity can be too much to bear. To avoid some of this I travel alone, without a publicity assistant to share my shame. This can, however, make one feel defenceless. I remember a recent visit to Glasgow, to do a reading in the Waterstone's there. As I was walking through the deserted shopping precinct I heard a voice hissing: 'You got a knife?' 'Actually, yes,' I replied. The man was sitting on the cobblestones, in the freezing cold, hunched over what looked like a pigeon. Peanuts lay scattered around. 'Help me, then,' he muttered. I took out my knife – a retractable blade I use to sharpen my eye-liner pencil – and gave it to him. Now I could see what he was doing: trying to cut some cotton thread that was tangled around the pigeon's leg. He tried to cut it, for some time. 'Steady me, can't you?' he said testily. 'Hold my shoulders!' I knelt down on the cobblestones and gripped his shoulders, as indicated. 'You'll have to throw this knife away afterwards,' he said, 'pigeons carry a disease that's fatal for humans.' This was rather a shame; I was fond of my knife and had never been able to find another one like it. As the minutes ticked by I said: 'I really ought to go, I'm a bit late.' 'Hang on!' he barked, busying himself with the purple, scabby leg of the pigeon. By this time I was really late and the pigeon's leg was still not freed. I told him to bring the knife to the bookshop down the road, walked there and started my reading. The audience consisted of four people, including a chap in an anorak who apparently came to all the readings with his mother and just wanted autographs. In the middle of my reading the door opened and the pigeon-liberator marched in, gave me back my knife and marched out again. I couldn't really explain to my audience what had happened. Besides, they were fast asleep.

There is much, much more. Bookshops where, when I enter and suggest signing some books, they look at me as if I've got dog's mess on my shoe. The audience on the *QE2* who sat there in silence and then, after half an hour, told me they were waiting to see the film *French Kiss* with Kevin Kline. An event at Edinburgh where, in front of a large audience, Hunter Davies' first question to me began: 'Well, Deborah Moggach, you're not really up there in the first eleven, are you?' A charity lunch which had cost me £120 in train fares and where my interviewer not only got my name wrong but called the novel I was going to be talking about (*The Ex-Wives*), 'The XYs' throughout, even though it was sitting there in front of her. The 'should I have heard of you's and the people who say 'you're my favourite writer' and then proceed to quote from someone else's book.

Novelists have an equivocal relationship with reality, as it is, and on a bad day we can feel as non-existent as the characters we have created – more so, sometimes. In my case this is compounded by the fact that I have never seen anyone reading any of my books, ever. Such a sight has occasionally been spotted, on buses or trains, but can one really believe this? After all, I spend my life making things up.

Still, mortification is something we feed off. We can use it in our work, just as we use everything else. And we know, deep down, that we deserve it. Every writer I know is waiting for the tap on the shoulder and the voice that says: 'So you really thought you could get away with it?'

'It matters not what you are thought to be, but what you are.'
Publilius Syrus

Thomas Lynch

It was in Aldeburgh in East Anglia at a poetry festival there where I first got a whiff of delectable celebrity. The airfare paid for by my publisher, the car and driver waiting at the train station, the posters with my photo and name in bold Garamond, the banner over the high street proclaiming the long weekend's literary events, the welcome from the festival committee and the chummy greetings of the other luminaries – each added a measure to the gathering sense of self-importance.

We all had put our public faces on. There was Paula Meehan from Dublin, Deryn Rees-Jones, a young and comely Liverpudlian, Charles Boyle, then a junior editor at Faber & Faber. I was the American with Irish connections whose day job as a funeral director struck folks as sufficiently odd to merit mention in the local press. The publication, the year before, of my first UK collection of poems meant that I was now on the record and ignored throughout the English-speaking world, my books for sale if unsold in Adelaide and Montreal, Wellington and Edinburgh, New York, Vancouver and London. We were all poets of the book or two-book sort, on the edge of greater greatness or obscurity, to whom the keys to this eastern seaside town had been given in the first week of November 1995 for the 7th Annual Aldeburgh International Poetry Festival. The tide of good fortune to which celebrities become accustomed was rising as we strolled the esplanade, Ms Meehan and me, talking of friends we shared in Ireland and America, the rush of the off-season surf noising in the shingle, the lights coming on in tall windows of the Victorian seafront lodges. At one corner, a pair of local spinsters standing in their doorway called us in to tea and talk of literary matters. They had prepared an elegant spread of finger foods and relevant questions about contemporary poetry and the bookish arts in general. We were, Paula and me, asked for what was reckoned expert testimony on verse and verse makers – the long-deceased and the more recently published. Then there were the panels and interviews, recorded for the local radio stations, and readings held in the Jubilee Hall, a vast brick warehouse that had been turned into a performance space by the installation of amphitheatric seating and microphones and stage lighting. The house was packed for every event, the sale of books was brisk, the lines at the signing tables long and kindly. They were so glad to meet us, so pleased to be a part of such a 'magical event'. The air was thick with superlative and serendipity, hyperbole and Ciceronian praise. And after every event the poets – myself among them – were invited to a make-shift canteen across the street above the town's cinema. Teas and coffees, soups and sandwiches, domestic and imported lagers, local cheeses and continental wines were put out for the hard-working and presumably ever hungry and thirsty poets who, for their part, seemed fashionably beleaguered and grateful for the afterglow among organizers and groupies. We were like rock-and-roll stars on tour, clasping our thin volumes and sheaves of new work like the instruments of our especial trade, basking in the unabashed approval of these locals and out-of-towners. It was all very heady and generous.

A poet far removed from his own country, I felt at last the properly appreciated prophet. For every word there seemed an audience eager to open their hearts and minds. Strangeness and distance made every utterance precious. For while the Irish and Welsh and Scots were very well treated, and the English writers held their own, I was an ocean and a fair portion of continent from home and made to feel accordingly exotic and, for the first time in my life, almost *cool*.

Home in Michigan a mortician who wrote poems was the social equivalent of a dentist who did karaoke: a painful case made more so by the dash of boredom. But here in England, I was not an oddity, but a celebrity, being 'minded' by a team of local literarians, smart and shapely women – one tendering a medley of local farm cheeses, another pouring a cup full of tea, another offering homemade scones, still another – the pretty wife of the parish priest – taking notes as I held forth in conversation with another poet on the metabolics of iambic pentameter and the 'last time I saw Heaney' or 'Les Murray' or some greater fixture in the firmament. And though I'd been, by then, abstemious for years, the star treatment was an intoxicant. The centre of such undivided attention, I became chatty and fashionably manic, conversationally nimble, intellectually vibrant, generous and expansive in every way, dizzy and dazzling to all in earshot, myself included.

So it was when I espied in the doorway of this salon a handsome man I recognized as someone I had seen before, I assumed he must be from Michigan, since this was my first time ever in these parts. His dress was more pressed and precise than any writerly type – more American – a memorable face with a forgettable name, possibly a Milfordian on holiday or a fellow Rotarian, or a funeral director whom I'd met at a national convention who, having read about my appearance in one of the English dailies, had paused in his tour to make his pilgrimage to Aldeburgh to hear me read. It was the only explanation. My memory of him, though incomplete, was unmistakable: I knew this pilgrim and not from here.

I excused myself from the discourse with the churchman's wife and made my way across the room to what I was sure would be his eager salutations. But he seemed to look right past me, as if he'd come for something or someone else. Perhaps, I thought, he did not recognize me out of my familiar surroundings and funereal garb. The closer I got the more certain I was that he and I shared an American connection. I rummaged through my memory for a bit of a name, or place or time on which to fix the details of our acquaintance.

'How good to see you!' I said. 'And so far from home!'

Fully fed on the rich fare of celebrity, I was expansive, generous, utterly sociable.

I took his hand and shook it manfully. He looked at me with genteel puzzlement.

'I know I know you but I can't say from where . . .' I said, certain that he would fill in the details . . . the friend we had in common, the event, the circumstances of his being here.

'Tom Lynch,' I smiled, 'from Michigan' and then, in case our connection was professional, 'from Lynch & Sons, in Milford.'

'How nice to meet you Mr Lynch. Fines . . . Ray Fines . . .' His voice was hesitant, velvety, trained; a clergyman I thought. They were always doing these 'exchanges' whereby one rector traded duties and homes for a season with another, the better to see the world on a cleric's stipend. Or a TV reporter, the UK correspondent for CNN perhaps, maybe wanting an interview with the visiting American poet?

'Are you here on holidays?' I asked him.

'No, no, just visiting friends.' He kept looking around the room as if I wasn't the reason for his being here.

'And where did we first meet? I just can't place it,' I said.

'I am certain I don't know,' he said, and then almost shyly, 'perhaps you have seen me in a movie.'

'Movie?'

'Yes, well, maybe,' he said. 'I act.'

It was one of those moments when we see the light or debouch from the fog into the focused fact of the matter. I had, of course, first seen him in America, in Michigan, in the Milford Cinema, where he'd been the brutal Nazi, Amon Goeth, who shoots Jews for sport in *Schindler's List* and more recently in *Quiz Show* where he'd played the brainy if misguided golden boy of the American poet, Mark Van Doren. He was not Ray Fines at all. He was *Ralph Fiennes*. His face was everywhere – the globalized image of mannish beauty in its prime, and dark thespian sensibility, privately desired by women on several continents and in many languages whilst here I was, slam-dunked in the hoop-game of celebrity before I'd even had a chance to shine. Across the room I could see the rector's wife, watching my encounter with the heartthrob. She was wide-eyed and blushing and expecting, I supposed, an introduction.

A contortionist of my acquaintance, whose name would not be recognized were I to use it, though he has accumulated some regional fame for something he does with thumbs, once theorized that if the lower lip could be stretched over one's head, and one could quickly swallow, one could disappear. Never had I a greater urge to test the theory than that moment in Aldeburgh.

'There are more ways of killing a dog than choking it with butter.'
Proverb

D.B.C. Pierre

The Art Beast spoke to me on the road to becoming a writer. It urged me to explore every opportunity for life experience, because as an artist it would be my job to probe the edges where others mightn't go. The taste of these edges must one day fly off a written page, said the Beast.

This was a bloody stupid thing to say to me.

I sometimes visited Australia in spring or autumn. This is when flies in the outback swarm fewer than eight deep to your nostrils, eyes, and mouth; an opportunity certain mates and I took as a mandate to pack a car with baked beans, port, and rifles, and drive across nowhere looking for animals to shoot. Hunting, we called it. Wild goat by day, fox by night, for these were introduced pests, doing violence to the balance of nature.

We never once suspected our testicles of contriving this excuse.

Conditions on these trips were traditionally cold and prickly. Then one day a mate secured a cautious invitation to use a distant relative's homestead as a base. The offer came after much lobbying of the mate's elders, the kind that don't answer when you ask them favours, that just sort of creak, or suddenly sneeze and have a stroke.

We leapt at the invitation, though it was made clear our host's property was a working farm; we would camp in the shearing shed, and our behaviour should be beyond reproach.

And so, while three city boys debated whether an ice-cream machine or a taco dinner kit would make a better gift for the host, our mate with the country connection quietly slung a sack of oranges into the car, and we drove one crisp evening with our guns and spotlights towards the back of beyond. Two-horse towns along the road became one-horse, then semi-horse, until finally no town slipped behind us.

We arrived next morning at the homestead of a sheep station that underlooked a rusty spine of mountains. A pair of large ears bobbed to the door, as if attached to the wrong farmer. We waited as the old boy scratched at a subdued flannel shirt beneath a dutifully knitted, and just as dutifully eroded woollen waistcoat, while his wife, a kindly wraith in combat boots, squeaked comfortingly in the dark behind him. Between them sat the family dog; a kelpie whose quicksilver eyes confirmed that he'd not only run the farm for the last decade, but was the only one in the house who knew how to work the video.

Then, carefully re-working the sixteen words that had formed their verbal life since the Great War – sensible, God-given words – the couple bade us welcome with such awkward charm that we felt like rocking them in our arms. We couldn't, obviously, due to country etiquette, which regarded even handshakes as perilously intimate. No, the protocols of out-back conversation demanded that we stand on the veranda, arms folded, and stare at the ground until we were shown to our quarters. The shed wasn't much, but it had a fireplace, and we were glad of that. It's much easier to fart competitively, and invent new words for genitalia, when not covered in frost.

We set out in camouflage later that day, the car a hedgehog of protruding gun barrels. But our plan to rid the world of evil hit a snag. Nothing of any size moved in the ranges, save the odd kangaroo. We would have to travel some distance, and beware of sheep resembling goats.

All alcohol had been left at the shed, that's how responsible we were, and we kept our guns unloaded in the car, except for one of the mates, Steve, whose name I should've withheld. He shot a hole through the roof as we bumped through a creek bed. I spent the rest of the day dissuading him from firing at parrots and crows.

Spiders and moths were in danger by the second day. A fur of bean skins upholstered our teeth, and clots of instant coffee in tepid rainwater failed to rinse away the sting of a cold night's sleep. We fell prey to goatlessness, goatlessness and foxlessness, in a big way. At home our women and peers would be waiting, not for triumphant hauls of game, but for their absence. They would be like that illusory strain of public opinion to which a government loses face if it recalls its troops unbloodied, having sent them primed for war.

The reckless eddies at death's edge sucked at us. Alright, at me.

On the last night we stayed out late, relentlessly spotlighting for so much as a rabbit. To no avail. God's creatures survived us. We finally turned the car toward the homestead, defeated.

Then, as we passed through the boundary fence, a pair of eyes flashed in the headlights. Textbook eyes, away in a far paddock. The spotlight burst back into life, weapons were quietly loaded. There it was. Fox. Check the ears. Unmistakable.

'Hang on,' said a voice of reason. 'We're in the homestead grounds . . .'

'Bang.' Too late. Eyes and ears dropped behind the grass.

We dispersed on foot to retrieve the kill. It was around here somewhere. Or maybe it was over there.

After two hours we still hadn't found the carcass. The spaces were wide and deceptive, it was dark. The animal may have been there, dead, hidden. Or horribly, unthinkably, it may have had life enough to crawl away and die.

So here, true mortification being such a personal, slow-dawning emotion, I abandon you to the interactive bosom of the written word for the tale's dread punch-line. Feel this one in your guts.

Next morning, the bright-eyed, spiky-eared, reddish-brown farm dog, the farmer's only friend and colleague – was nowhere to be found.

'Hay is more acceptable to an ass than gold.' Latin proverb

Val McDermid

Writing genre fiction is a calling more prone to humiliation than most fields of creative endeavour. Yes, we face the same rejections from agents and publishers, the mortification of being asked if we write under our own names, the shame of events where only two people turn up. But we also face the indignity of being one of a bunch in the review section's crime round-up. And possibly worst of all, the perennial question: 'Have you ever thought of writing a proper novel?'

You'd think after fifteen years, nearly twenty novels and a slew of awards I'd be inured to it. But it still stings to be treated like the unfortunate member of the family who's a bit mentally defective.

Picture the scene. A Sunday morning at one of the country's most prestigious literary festivals. To protect the guilty, let's call it Wheat-on-Rye. I had crawled out of bed at the crack of dawn to drive myself and a fellow crime writer from Manchester to the middle of nowhere to take part in a panel with a literary novelist who had written a novel that 'subverted the conventions of the crime novel'. We're used to this sort of thing. It usually translates as, 'I'm a literary novelist, so it doesn't matter if my detective procedure bears no relationship to reality and my plot has more holes than Blackburn, Lancashire, because I am writing deep and meaningful prose.'

With some misgivings, we settled down in front of a packed house. The moderator's first question was to my colleague. 'So, you write about a police officer. Do you actually spend time with real police officers to find out about their work?' Next question to me. 'You've written about a psychological profiler. You must have had to do a lot of research to find out how they do the job.' And to the literary writer? 'You're clearly very concerned with language and style. What made you want to experiment with form in this way?'

And so it continued. Patronizing questions to the crime writers that allowed little or no discussion of our craft or the wider ideas that inform our work. No suggestion that we might be writing something that went beyond the crossword puzzle with the neat resolution. And fawning questions about literature and society to the literary novelist (actually a rather nice man who had the grace to look embarrassed about the whole thing . . .).

By the end of the panel, I was inches away from physical assault on the moderator, who was only saved by the Q&A session. The audience at least understood that crime fiction as it is currently practised is light years away from Agatha Christie and Dorothy L. Sayers, and asked the sort of questions a reasonable moderator might have thought of. By the end of the hour, my blood pressure had almost reached normal levels.

But as usual, just when you think it's safe to go in the water, something comes up and bites you on the bum. We were whisked away from our tent to the Green Room. As we entered, our festival escort drew in her breath sharply. There, sitting round the central coffee table, was a group that included Stephen Fry, Michael Ignatieff and Steven Berkoff. Clearly, we couldn't be allowed to contaminate such an intellectual gathering. So with breathtaking chutzpah, she steered the scuzzy crime writers away from the heart of the room to a little table in the corner where we could wait for our fee without tainting the high tone of the gathering.

Really, I was astonished that we were paid our fee in champagne. Given the flavour of the rest of the morning I fully expected a crate of brown ale.

'A fly, Sir, may sting a stately horse and make him wince; but one is but an insect, and the other is a horse still.' Samuel Johnson

William Boyd

The writer is on leg four of his seven-leg book tour of the USA. He has done New York, Washington DC and Boston and is about to head for Cleveland, Ohio, when he receives the bad news. His latest, ambitious, big novel has received a lengthy, sniffy review in the Sunday book section of the *New York Times*. Even on the telephone he can sense the awful plunge in morale at his American publishers: the gloom is palpable, bitter disappointment practically drips from the telephone receiver. For a foreign writer in America there is really only one review that counts: the *New York Times* Sunday book supplement. If that's bad, to put it bluntly, then everything else – including all the other good reviews this book has had – is a waste of time and such is the implicit message relayed to him by his suicidal editor. The writer thinks to himself – as he boards the plane to Cleveland, Ohio – that, if indeed this is the case, then what the hell is he doing on a book tour across the USA? Why is he flying thousands of miles to Cleveland and Seattle and San Francisco and Los Angeles? Why doesn't

he just go home? The writer was me; the date was 1988 and
the book was my novel *The New Confessions*, a near 500-page
fake autobiography of a Scottish film-maker who throughout
his long life is driven to try and film *The Confessions* of Jean-
Jacques Rousseau.

At Cleveland airport I am met by my 'escort', whom we
shall call 'Phyllis'. Phyllis is the wife of a lawyer or a dentist
or a doctor. She loves books and she drives a big expensive
car. As the writer travels across America he is met in each city
by reproductions of these benign matrons who will shepherd
him from hotel to book-signing to radio station to lunch with
a journalist. They are kind and well-meaning: the relationship
is of aunt to favourite, talented nephew (or niece). They are
rooting for you. Phyllis checks me into my anonymous hotel
in downtown Cleveland. I say I will order from room service
for my evening meal. She runs through my schedule: an early
rise for a radio show then to a TV station for a breakfast show,
then a tour of bookshops before I catch a midday plane for
San Francisco, or is it Seattle? See you tomorrow at 6.00 a.m.
Phyllis says, and then adds that she's started my book and is
loving it.

I order a club sandwich from room service and drink
steadily from the mini-bar while watching some TV. I think
about going down to the hotel bar; I think about going out
for a stroll; I decide to stay in my acceptable room. Literature?
– I'm in it for the glamour.

In the early morning sunshine Phyllis drives me through
Cleveland's outer suburbs. I get glimpses of the enormous
inland sea that is Lake Erie. Every house we pass seems to
possess three cars and a boat of some description. This radio
station appears to be miles away.

Eventually we find it – like a clapboard bungalow with a

thirty-foot aerial set at the apex of its roof. The interviewer is a genial, bearded man. In between MOR standards he asks me questions about the Royal Family and London's notorious pea-souper fogs. He makes great play with the fact that I have the same name as the actor who was TV cowboy Hopalong Cassidy. He also uses me to introduce the ad breaks. 'Do you like potato chips, William?' 'I do,' I confess, 'but we call them "crisps" in England.' He repeats the word several times, rolling the 'r'. 'Then I think you'd like these American potato chips, too.' In the course of our interview I similarly endorse Shake 'n' Vac carpet cleaner ('Do your carpets ever get dirty, William?') and a brand of motor oil.

That went great, Phyllis enthuses, as we drive to the TV station. Here in the green room I am offered coffee and muffins and am introduced to the other breakfast guests: an enormous young man, whose back is the size of a kitchen table and whose neck is thicker than his head, and a little girl in a pink dress who's accompanied by her awestruck parents. The little girl goes on first, followed by me, then the giant.

By now I'm on a form of auto-pilot and am strangely calm as an assistant producer tells me that the little girl has won some high-school spelling bee and that the giant is a footballing superstar from a local college team, the Spartans or the Mavericks – I don't take it in. 'Could you tell us a little about your book, William?' the producer asks, pen poised. I decide not to mention Jean-Jacques Rousseau.

I greet my hosts on the stage as we wait for the weather report to be read and the little girl is led off. 'Isn't she cute?' Very cute, I concur. The male and female hosts look impossibly healthy, creaselessly neat. 'You know you have the same name as Hopalong Cassidy?' the man says. 'You got your horse tied up outside?' I laugh along with them both.

We're on air. 'Our next guest today is British writer William Boyd with his latest book *True Confessions*. Morning, William.' I say good morning back. 'So, William,' the woman presenter asks me, 'tell me all about your Princess Diana.'

That went great, Phyllis enthuses, as we drive to the first of three bookshops I will sign stock in. I duly meet the earnest, amiable booksellers who sympathize about the *New York Times* review ('Shame about the *Times*') but who congratulate me on my morning TV appearance. Everyone agrees it's great publicity. Great publicity for the British Royal Family, I reflect, as I sign a dozen books in each shop before Phyllis says we're running late and had better race for the airport.

I assure Phyllis she doesn't need to check me in, that I can manage the task myself, unsupervised. So we make our farewells at Departures. 'Oh my God, I almost forgot!' she says reaching into the glove compartment for a copy of my book. I think of the cities up ahead waiting for me and I want to go home. 'For Phyllis,' I write, knowing it's not her fault, 'thanks for everything.'

'The artist cannot get along without a public; and when the public is absent, what does he do? He invents it, and turning his back on his age, he looks toward the future for what the present denies.'
André Gide

William Trevor

Search childhood for those undying harvests of humiliation and faithfully they come scuttling back. In weary tones of classroom despair, the careless arrows are still cast, *V. Poor* inscribed a thousand times. 'You wrote a poem,' a voice calls down the table while teatime sausage-rolls are passed along the rows. Surreptitiously written, surreptitiously delivered to I.G. Sainsbury, more man than boy, editor of the subversive magazine. 'How did you know?' I whisper beneath the clatter of feet as we leave the dining hall, and learn that Sainsbury needed something to light his cigarette with.

Employment nurtured more of the same. But when the years begin to pile up, mockery loses its sting, as if it has done with you at last; and matters less, then not at all. What follows now should have been a mortification, yet wasn't when it happened.

I received a letter from the Arts Council informing me that I had been awarded a literary prize and binding me to secrecy until after the presentation. In due course there was a

telephone call from the Arts Council's public relations department, with details of a few publicity wheezes that might be put
in place then too. I explained that I wasn't good on publicity
but agreed to give a reading. This was to be an item in an
arts festival which by coincidence would be in full swing in
and around London at the same time. The Thames was mentioned when I asked and I thought of Marlow, or Hampton
perhaps.

It turned out to be neither. On the evening after the award
ceremony my wife and I met a young man from the festival
and an attractive lady from the Arts Council in the hall of
Durrant's Hotel, where we all waited for the taxi that was to
take us to our rendezvous. 'And where exactly is that?' I asked
and was told it was the Thames Flood Barrier. Agitated telephone calls were made when our taxi didn't arrive. When it
still didn't we picked one up on the street.

We crawled through heavy traffic, taking longer about it
than our minders had intended. Meditating on which bridge
to cross, the driver took the opportunity to enquire if we were
certain that the Flood Barrier was where we wanted to go,
since at this time of night there mightn't be much doing out
there. We reassured him and he drove patiently on, identifying
for us the impressive riverside buildings when at last we
reached them. In time we left Southwark behind, and Ber-
mondsey and Deptford. A sign to Greenwich looked promis-
ing, but stylish Greenwich wasn't for us. We'd been on the
road for more than an hour when we turned out of the traffic,
into docklands that for the most part were pitch-dark.

'Well, now you've got me,' the taxi-driver confessed, his
headlights sweeping over a vast concrete nowhere, roadless
and signless. 'I have a telephone number,' the young man said.

As he spoke, two figures were suddenly lit up, gazing at

our approach. They were schoolgirls, who asked us when we stopped if we were Gilbert and George. We said we weren't and they despondently wandered off into the dark again.

We drove on, windows down, all of us peering out. 'That could be a telephone box,' someone said, and it was. We drew up beside it and watched the young man prodding in his number and then waiting to be answered. We heard a very faint ringing that ceased when he put the receiver down. We passed this on to him when he returned to the taxi and he hammered on the door of what in the glow from the telephone-box appeared to be a shed. Nothing happened, so we all got out except the taxi-driver.

A touch of fog had developed and we made our way cautiously through it, aware of architectural shapes that were not quite buildings, and of silence and the rawness of the air. As we turned to go back to the taxi, shadows moved in the far distance and, while we watched, three tall men materialized. They were carrying soundboxes and other electrical equipment; behind them there was a woman with two plates of sandwiches. Someone had seen a car driving about, she said.

We followed them and the taxi followed us. The doors of a building that had eluded us before were unlocked, lights came on and we went in. Chairs were arranged in rows but no one was sitting on them. 'What's going to happen now?' the taxi-driver wanted to know, keen for more adventure. He was surprised when I said I was going to read a story but, obliging as ever, he sat down in the front row with some of the sandwiches. Then a boy and his father joined him. Reading it, I made the story rather shorter than it was.

As we passed the schoolgirls on our way back to central London we offered them a lift but they were suspicious and refused. Gilbert and George hadn't felt like performing artistically in a waterworks was what they reckoned, and said with some feeling that they didn't blame them.

The taxi-driver drew up in Wigmore Street, where the young man visited a hole-in-the-wall before attempting to settle the taxi bill. 'Come in and have a drink,' I invited him and the Arts Council lady when we reached Durrant's Hotel. I invited the taxi-driver too because he'd been so nice, but he said he'd better not. I signed the story I'd read and gave it to him instead.

Over drinks, I dismissed what signs there were that apologies might be in order. Blame does not belong when the circumstances are flawed and in the warm, snug bar it seemed neither here nor there that twenty-four hours hadn't been time enough to spread the word of a forthcoming event; neither here nor there that the docklands at night were perhaps not quite the place for Gilbert and George's subtleties. As for us, our evening out couldn't be decribed as anything less than grist to the fiction-writer's mill; and more enjoyable – although I didn't say it – than the tedium of what might have been.

'The critic's pretence that he can unravel the procedure is grotesque. As well hope to start with a string of sausages and reconstruct the pig.' B.H. Streeter

Julie Myerson

The world is divided into novelists who do and novelists who don't. I don't blame the ones who don't: it's not well-paid and it's the quickest way to make enemies this side of the divorce courts. Incest some people call it, others denounce you as a hack. Why, they ask, just because you write books, should you want to review them? But if you write fiction yourself, I'd reply, what could possibly be more satisfying and exciting than the chance to respond in print to the work of your contemporaries? At its best, it's an exhilarating exercise, attempting to explore in words why a novel scorched your heart.

I always do think of it as a response, not a judgement. Part of a feisty, ongoing dialogue – words fired at words. But I know I'm fooling myself. The dialogue can quickly turn to war. So I'm careful. I don't review my friends or authors whose work I already know I don't like. And I start every novel with a sense of hope. But then sometimes, for all your optimism, you just don't like it. And then, yes, you have to say so. But as a novelist myself – who knows how it feels to have your life-force sucked out by the crushing power of a bad review – how do I ever justify pulling another author's work apart?

Well, my theory is that if you dish it out (criticism that is), then you've simply got to be able to take it. So I made two rules for myself:

1. Read every review, even the good ones, once and only once – then file and forget.
2. Be very nice to People Who've Given You Bad Reviews. Shock them into liking you. Make them regret what they wrote!

And have I stuck to The Myerson Rules? Well, there was the dinner party where I realized as I walked in that the woman whose hand I was about to shake had given me The Worst Review I've Ever Had. Not just bad but personal too – she'd made assumptions about the rest of my work (and its apparently undeserved success) based on the one slim tome she'd read. Voodoo pins were not agonizing enough for this woman.

But had I read her review just the once? Hmmm. That's a tricky one. I do know that as I was introduced to her, all her weasel words came sneaking back. But, I rallied, it's a whole lot worse for her than for me. So I stuck to Rule Number 2. I never (of course) referred to her (ludicrous) review. I made as if I'd forgotten it completely. Instead I told her how much I liked her last book (unutterably dull), how interesting her new one (verging on pointless) sounded. I dazzled her, I flattered her – actually I think I scared her! A few days later, my reward plopped through the door: a sweet, hand-written letter from her apologizing for the original review. Two years too late perhaps, but hell, I wasn't complaining. One Nil.

Sometimes as a critic you just take a deep breath and hope the author doesn't remember it was you. I was sitting next to a really nice young man at a literary lunch, a formal affair with silver cutlery and waiters and a seating plan. 'Why do I know your name?' I asked him over and over as I stared at his place-card.

'Oh,' he said vaguely, 'I write a kind of a column for . . .' He named the paper.

'No,' I said, 'I never see that paper. It's not that. This is really getting to me. I'm convinced I know you from somewhere.'

After half an hour of this (me digging deeper, him frantically filling the hole), the poor man lit a cigarette and gave in.

'Well,' he said rather sheepishly, 'I think I reviewed one of your novels. I mean – I know I did.'

I beamed at him. 'Oh – well then!'

'It wasn't a very good review,' he muttered quickly, 'in fact it was rather scathing. I'm so sorry.'

I don't know what he expected me to do. Move table? Slap him Bette Davis-style across the cheek? Break down and sob? No, I laughed and told him that it was quite alright. I told him that I think Authors Learn From Their Bad Reviews. 'Quite often as the months or years go by, you realize a certain critic's response was right, more or less.'

He looked relieved. 'Really? You really mean that?'

I nodded sweetly.

Did I mean it? Did I really? Let's put it this way: I tried very hard to. I still do. And this so-called reviewer and I got on extremely well and by the end of the lunch were the firmest of friends. I still know him. Last year he invited me to his birthday party. Two Nil. (So there's another critic who's going to have to think twice before dissing one of my books ever again.)

'Hell is full of musical amateurs: music is the brandy of the damned.' Shaw, *Man and Superman*

James Lasdun

Mortification: the default mode of anyone involved in writing or other forms of self-exhibition, deliberate or accidental. Like the time I was sitting naked on the toilet of an outdoor portaloo at a racecourse, when all four doors spontaneously collapsed outward to reveal Her Majesty the Queen and the entire royal family staring at me in horror as I relieved myself . . . Oh, but that was a dream, of course, and yet how natural it felt; how strangely true to life – my life at any rate. And the fact is, when it comes to real mortification, the kind where you spiral inward past the circumstances themselves, and sink into the deep dark matter of your own psyche, it can be hard to tell whether you're awake or dreaming.

At school, when I was seventeen, I had a band. That is to say I had a shiny red Gibson SG copy, a wah-wah pedal, an amp, and a couple of friends with similarly noisy pieces of equipment. On weekends we'd score a bag of ganja, lay in some fine barley wines, get good and smashed, and start jamming.

That summer the school decided to honour its growing contingent of young rockers with an afternoon concert. Nobody had heard our band play, but this, combined with our generally stoned demeanour, merely added to our mystique. We were called 'Barbarossa's Body'; I don't remember why, but I do remember overhearing some juniors who passed us in a corridor whisper admiringly: *They're Barbarossa's Body; they're playing in the concert,* and feeling rather grand.

The time for the concert drew near. I prepared for it by buying an afghan sheepskin waistcoat on the Portobello Road. It was embroidered with silk stars and small mirrors, and bordered all around with long, thick, yellowish-grey sheep hair which, particularly at the armholes, where it sprouted out like two enormous shaggy sunflowers, gave me a primitive appearance that I found pleasing.

At lunchtime on the day of the concert itself, I felt suddenly unwell. So unwell that I had to be excused from the table to get a breath of fresh air. I'd never gone on stage before, and it hadn't occurred to me to get nervous, but as I walked across the schoolyard, I realized I was suffering from an anxiety so acute it was making me nauseous. There was something else too. I couldn't quite put my finger on it, but it was giving me the dim feeling that something in my life was going truly, catastrophically wrong.

In this uncertain condition I put on my new waistcoat and went to meet my band backstage. The group before us did rockabilly covers – efficient, fast, and much appreciated by the audience. We took the stage. As we stood there looking at each other in our magnificent outfits, with waves of joyous expectation streaming up at us from the audience, there was a moment where reality seemed on the brink of miraculously breaking its own laws in order to conform with the infantile fantasies of effortless brilliance and adulation that had brought us up here. And then the little detail I had managed to overlook or suppress all this time, namely that we knew *not one single* song, that we barely knew which way up to hold our instruments, that our 'jam' sessions had been about on the level of children flying imaginary airplanes, swung suddenly into the foreground of my mind. In a blind panic I began thrashing at my guitar. My friends did likewise. There were a few seconds of puzzled silence in the hall. Then, like a coordinated wave going through a soccer crowd, the expressions on our audience's faces changed as one from bewilderment to incredulity to savage hilarity, and our cacophony was drowned out by the most powerfully demoralizing sound I had ever heard: the sound of five hundred schoolboys booing. Astonishing to relate, we didn't immediately give up. As if this reaction were not quite enough to gratify my apparently bottomless need for humiliation, not enough to acquire permanent mortification status as an event capable of turning me scarlet whenever I should happen to think of it in later life, I had to go up to the mike and make a bleating plea to the audience to 'give us a chance'. That done, I maxed the volume on my guitar for another thunderburst, this time pumping furiously on the wah-wah pedal, as if I could reverse the situation through sheer noise and will power, only to be greeted by a still more appalling sound than before: the audience's boos had turned to *baas*. My friends, getting the joke, and no doubt seeing an opportunity to salvage their own reputations, pointed at my sheepskin waistcoat, burst into treacherous laughter, and fled.

Mortify: to deprive of life; to kill, put to death (OED). In the sepulchral inner space I entered then, I understood one very simple thing: either the world was going to have to cease to exist, or else I myself was. No doubt the mark of a genius (or a madman) at such a juncture would be to choose the former. I didn't: I died. And what I think of now as I see myself standing there dumbstruck in my furry pelt, is the poor sheep Abraham put to death in his son Isaac's stead. My primordial sheep-self had been sacrificed in order that my new, cautious, responsible, realistic, adult self might be given life.

At any rate, I have made it a point, since then, to have a little something prepared on the rare occasions when I have to get up on a stage and perform.

'I have often lamented that we cannot close our ears with as much ease as we can our eyes.' Richard Steele

Maggie O'Farrell

The room is tiny. There are no windows and as far as I know the door may be locked from the outside. On the miniature, doll-sized desk in front of me are two pieces of chalk, a roll of gaffer tape and a razor blade. Strange acts have been committed here, by extremely small people. A man with a body odour problem has just come in and snapped a pair of excruciatingly tight headphones over my ears.

I hate doing live radio. I loathe and detest it. I don't even like talking on the phone, let alone doing an interview down a wire, with someone I can't see and have never met. I'm always convinced it will bring out my long-dormant stammer. And then there's the horrifying idea that people might be out there listening, from their cars, offices and kitchens. None of them, I am sure, will have the slightest interest in anything I have to say. Why have I agreed to this? What conspiracy of decisions or chains of events has brought me here, to this, sitting obediently in a head-manacle in a broom cupboard, sweating into my beloved best shirt, waiting for a sign from someone or something?

A trickle of notes down the line heralds my connection to the distant radio station, across the breadth of the country. A soupy jazz record is playing. I strain for the voice of a technician, telling me what's about to happen, but instead, over the tinkly piano, I hear the presenter yell, 'Who've we got next?'

There is a pause. A scuffling of papers. I sit up straighter, even though they can't see me, just to be ready.

'Eh . . .' another voice says over more paper-scuffling, '. . . Maggie O'Farrell.'

'Who?' the presenter barks.

'She's a writer.'

'For fuck's sake,' he yells, 'who booked her? I've never heard of her.'

I stop sitting straighter. Some part of me realizes that at this point I should cough or clear my throat to let them know that I'm here, but the presenter is still shouting:

'I'm sick of you booking these bloody nobodies. When are you going to get me some proper guests?'

The headphones are so tight I feel as though I'm undergoing a cranial lobotomy. I gaze blankly at the razor blade as the presenter harangues the producer for his bad choice in guests, demanding to know what my books are called, what they're about and what on earth I'm going to want to say.

'And where is she, anyway?' he snaps.

'She's in the other studio,' the producer says.

There is another pause while the jazz record spirals on, the pianist still tinkling away politely. We listen to each other breathing. The producer, poor man, clears his throat. 'Are you there, Maggie?'

'Yes,' I say.

'Can you hear us?' he asks weakly.

'Uh-huh.'

The record ends. The presenter fills his lungs. 'And now I have a special treat for you all. Here in the studio to talk about her new book is authoress Mary Farrell.'

'To have great poets, there must be great audiences too.'
Walt Whitman

Paul Muldoon

Worst of all, surely, was the occasion on which I set out by
train from New York City to read at a university one or two
states up the track. The university should remain nameless,
though if I were to mention its name you'd probably never
have heard of it. It was not a university of the first water, one
might say. I alighted at the station, expecting to be met, though,
since the arrangements had been made a good month earlier,
I began to doubt my memory of them. I waited long enough
for a little dusting of snow, then took a cab to the campus.
Nondescript is too colourful a word. I was carrying a letter
from my host which gave his office building and number. I
found my way to his door. No response. At least not from
him. There was, rather, the scraping of a chair from the next
office. Its inhabitant appeared. Professor So-and-so? There was
a glance over the shoulder, a shaking of the head. Professor
So-and-so had been on a three-week-long bender. Dreadful.
In a moment of lucidity, however, Professor So-and-so had
been in touch with the departmental secretary and had let her

know that an announcement of my reading should be made. This had happened as recently as yesterday. There hadn't, alas, been much time to run up a flyer. He rustled a khaki invitation which had already been all but obscured by an 'Anxious? Depressed? Suicidal?' poster.

Not to worry. Rough with the smooth. Hang loose. Stiff upper lip. The neighbour had to rush, alas, but he pointed me in the direction of the room in which the reading was meant to take place and informed me of the location of the hotel into which I'd been booked for the night. Needless to say, no arrangements had been made for my fee. Such considerations are not uppermost in the mind of someone committed to a three-week-long bender. The cheque would be in the mail. No need to worry about the hotel. That would be billed directly to the department. I agreed with the neighbour that it would probably have been better if someone had been available to give an introduction but, under the circumstances, I also had to agree with him that no introduction is better than one hastily cobbled together. I thanked him for his trouble and assured him I was perfectly happy to take things from there. I treated myself to a pizza in the student cafeteria and made my way to the room for a quarter to seven. The reading was due to start at seven and I was gratified to discover that there was already a core of five or six audience members. There to get a good seat, one would have thought, though they were all somehow huddled at the back. The core audience turned out to be the entire audience. Okay. Still better, I always think, than that time in the Moy when Jimmy Simmons and I read to his wife, my father, and my sister. At about five minutes past seven I got up and launched into my first poem. It was met with smiles and glances. They liked me. They really liked me. The second poem was guaranteed to knock them dead.

But just before I'd got to the end, one of my fans put up her hand and asked me how long I expected to be. What? The thing was, these students were involved in a study group and had settled in this empty classroom in the hope of finding a little peace and quiet.

I made my way to the hotel. Nondescript would definitely be too colourful, though the pillowcase had a scent which, to borrow a line of MacNeice, 'reminded [me] of a trip to Cannes'. At about four in the morning I awoke to find myself vigorously scratching myself here, there and everywhere. Reddish lumps here, there and everywhere. Fleas. I myself hopped out of bed and took the first train back to New York City.

'Better a quiet death than a public misfortune.' Spanish proverb

André Brink

This goes back a good number of years, when I was a young and eager writer (I'm still eager, but not quite so young), anxious to make a good impression, and only too conscious of the value of meeting the right people. I'm not normally all that eager to meet people, right or wrong, but it had been impressed upon me that this was the Right Thing To Do. So when I received the invitation to the birthday party of a Quite Important Publisher in Cape Town, I grimly resolved to go. Not so much for the sake of the birthday man himself as to meet another publisher who, I had been told by friends in the know, was just the man I should entrust my writing future to. I had a newly-completed manuscript, and this was the moment to decide its – and my – fate.

The evening started off on an uncomfortable note. The writer who had organized the gathering was known as a queer bird, as egocentric as they come; he had arranged it in what was undoubtedly the top hotel in town, and had in fact checked in a few days earlier (on the publisher's expense account) to make sure that everything would be Just So. He had chosen the menu (which meant all his own favourite dishes), ordered the wine (not so much by label as by price tag), picked two or three people who would ensure, unobtrusively but with great sophistication, that everything would Run Smoothly. When the guests arrived, he was there to look them over from a distance, and once everybody who Mattered had arrived, he haughtily withdrew to his room upstairs where, we learned later, he dined in solitary splendour, leaving the rest of us to our joint and several pursuits.

I am rather allergic to large gatherings of strangers, and hovered mostly on the periphery of the lively group in which everybody, except me, appeared to know everybody else. I managed to chat to a few people who seemed vaguely familiar, but they soon drifted off to what was, no doubt, more lively or more profitable conversation. I was left to myself, trying with as much enthusiasm as I could muster to enter into a passionate relationship with my glass of wine.

And then, suddenly, through some cosmic prestidigitation, the man appeared beside me. The Publisher. The One. I could not but recall a rather obvious graffito on the wall of a public toilet in São Paolo which had confidently informed me that, 'You are holding your future in your hands.'

I engaged The Man in conversation. Amazingly, he seemed interested in what I had to say. It became animated. All diffidence and anxiety left me. This was Going Well. Only, after a while it began to flag. I noticed that his eyes were wandering. He was looking for a new partner in conversation. I simply had to find something to keep him there, even if just for a few minutes, until the moment was ripe to broach the matter of my manuscript.

Looking round frantically in search of something to say, I

noticed at the far end of the bustling room a rather heart-rending sight: a woman on her own, clearly out of her depth, in clothes that simply did nothing for her at all. Feigning sophisticated sympathy, I turned to The Publisher, pointed in the direction of the ungainly female apparition, and asked, 'Who on earth is that wretched-looking woman over there?'

For some reason there seemed to appear a lull in the hubbub around us, as if not only The Man, but everybody, was listening to us.

And The Publisher said in very clearly demarcated words, each stressed separately, 'It is my wife.'

'The idea that the media is there to educate us, or to inform us, is ridiculous because that's about tenth or eleventh on their list. The first purpose of the media is to sell us shit.' Abbie Hoffman

Duncan McLean

On the whole, professional writers are a lot of whingeing bastards who wouldn't last a day in a real job. They get flown around the world for launches and festivals, treated to meals out and free room service, then have the gall to moan that their hotel's only four-star. They get off with translators, post-grad students and easily impressed publisher's publicists, then complain because only seventy-three of the seventy-six folk who struggled through the blizzard to attend their in-store reading loved them enough to actually buy the book. Of course I include myself in this miserable roll-call of inadequate no-lifers. Is my writing autobiographical? Yes it fucking is, for once.

The true mortification of being a writer is having to meet other writers from time to time, and listen to their mundane egotistical rantings. Like the ones I'm going to scratch down now about a typically humiliating day in a promotional tour I was asked to do a couple of years ago. The place: a large college town in the south-western USA. The start time: 7.14am.

Breakfast TV. Very like you'd imagine (so why waste words?), with the writer sandwiched on the mauve couch between a diet guru ('Fruits of the Desert weightloss plan – store those nutrients like a cactus') and the Texoma spelling-bee champ, muttering between her braces, 'Chrysanthemum, ineradicable, diarrhoea . . .'

The host was plump and shiny. An assistant dashed in during the ad breaks to dab his sweat away. His left shoelace was undone and trailing.

'And we're back,' he said. 'Our guest today has written a novel called *Bunker Man*. What's that all about?'

'Golf,' I said, smiling broadly. 'Witty repartee in the sand trap.'

His face brightened. 'Really?'

'No, but I thought you'd like that more than a psychosexual horror story full of squalid under-age copulation in a concrete bomb-shelter.'

'You're right,' he said.

During the phone-in section of the show there were quite a few callers for the 'Have you ever seen a fat cactus?' guru, but only one for me: 'Dance with the one who brung you,' said the voice over the monitor.

'Pardon?' I said.

'You haven't mentioned this evening's sponsor once, and we're paying for free beverages until eleven. Show some gratitude! And there's not nearly as much golf in your book as we were led to believe . . .'

'Thank you so much,' said the host, sweating again. 'Next!'

'Diarrhoea?'

Next stop was a lunchtime reading and signing at a big chain in a big mall in a big retail park on the edge of town. There was no one there. Not just no audience for me, but no customers at all. And no staff either. Well, there had to be someone somewhere: otherwise, who had pressed *play* on the CD of Boston Pops covers of Billy Joel's greatest hits?

Eventually I managed to find a cash-desk, where HI I'M CLEBO (according to his lapel badge) looked astonished when I introduced myself.

'I guess it was Appalachia who booked you, was it?'

'I don't know. I just got given this list of places to show up to . . .'

'May I see? Oh . . . yeah. That is us. What's the date?'

'The fourteenth.'

'That's what it says here.'

'I know. That's why I came today.'

'But this is Appalachia's day off.'

'Oh. So?'

'Nobody's here. Usually we have great turnouts. On Thursday we had over two hundred for . . .'

'Never mind, never mind; could I just sign some stock for you?'

'Eh . . .'

'Listen, I've come all the way from Scotland, the least I could do is . . .'

'Yeah yeah. Help yourself.'

'Well. Where is it?'

'Oh. What do you write?'

'Novels, mostly.'

'You mean fiction?'

'Eh . . . aye. Yes.'

'Down that aisle, past reflexology and area cuisine. It's in-back of quilting.'

I detoured to the coffee shop annexe, picked up a frozen

cappuccino, and eventually tracked down my books. There were two of them, two copies of the last book I'd published. They didn't have any of the new one I was meant to be promoting. Ah well. I signed them anyway, then signed the dozen or so Norman Macleans just to the right. I was going to start on Ed McBain, but noticed he had three full shelves all to himself . . .

Suddenly exhausted, I slumped down in a mauve armchair and studied my itinerary. (How my little heart had raced with pride and excitement when it'd been faxed through to me back home in Scotland! With the famous New York publisher's logo at the top of the page and its list of cities from the Chuck Berry songbook, all pantingly awaiting my arrival!) I had four hours till the next event: a buffet at the home of the night's sponsor, a nightclub owner. It'd be my chance, I'd been told, to visit with the people who'd subscribed to a series of literary readings, subsidizing my travel and hotel.

'You're going to have to sing for your supper,' said the organizer. 'While the guests are eating, I want you to sit at the end of the table and perform for us. One of your stories. Maybe that really funny one where the lovers think they don't have enough money for food, so they go out and shoplift their breakfast.'

'They don't *think* they've got no money,' I'd said, 'they really don't.'

'That's the one,' she said. 'Hilarious.'

The nightclub gig began about ten. I was to be on last: the visiting celebrity reader. A celebrity because I was visiting, no other reason. It seemed I was the only one reading here for the first time. In fact I was the only one reading who hadn't read here every Saturday night for the past year.

What this meant was, I was the only one turning up with a

selection of subtly-nuanced Chekhovian tales of life in the dull, heart-withering badlands of a knackered northern country. Everyone else came armed with a cartload of rock-sized poems or raps, mostly centred on fist fights, methadone addiction, penis size (especially as related to other male readers present), whisky vomit, male rape, blackouts, death (especially as imagined for all other readers present), your mutha, your sista, your muthafucking sista, and the price of beer in the student union.

There was two hours of this, with me pinned back against the mauve leather banquette by the amplified torrent of screamed words from the stage, most of them (it seemed) directed to me, the upstart muthafucking so-called celebrity no one had fucking heard of. I'd just decided to abandon my policy of sipping from a single bottle of beer all night (in order to retain professionally crisp enunciation when I was finally on stage) in favour of a more appropriate bottle-of-Jim-Beam-down-in-one approach, when I heard my name being screamed out. I jumped up.

'Hello,' I said. 'I thought I'd start with an excerpt from my new novel. It's a psychosexual horror story full of squalid under-age copulation and lunatic rantings . . .'

There was a howl from the darkness.

'Pardon?'

'No!' came a yell from the depths. 'We want to hear your golf stories.'

What could I do? What do you think, for Christ's sake? Like any good professional writer, paying for their fifty weeks of solitary deskbound scribbling in the only way possible – i.e. by whoring themselves to anyone anywhere willing to buy a plane ticket and a chance to shift a few units – I gave them the fucking golf story.

'The tongue is more to be feared than the sword.' Japanese proverb

Vicki Feaver

I'd gone into schools before and enjoyed it. The teachers were welcoming and friendly; the children enthusiastic about writing poetry with a 'real' poet. But this school, a boy's comprehensive, was different. The Head of English was surly and suspicious. He didn't introduce me to any of the other teachers. He didn't tell me anything about the boys I was to work with: just gave me the class registers with strict instructions to fill them in. Obviously, he didn't want me there. Maybe he thought poets were anarchists.

'We don't accept any work that contains sex or violence,' he said.

The classroom he led me to was right at the back of the school with windows facing north. The walls were bile yellow as if to compensate for the lack of sun. There was a smell of boiled cabbage and toilets. As soon as he'd gone, I stood on a chair to open a window. Then a bell rang and the first group of boys burst in. There were catcalls and wolf-whistles.

'Great view of your knickers, Miss,' a boy called out.

Certainly, the boys were interested in sex. 'Have you got a boyfriend? Is he good in bed?' was a running gag. I thought of getting them to write a sestina with that as one of the recurring lines; but resisted it.

There were five groups altogether, ranging in age from eleven to fifteen: all equally unruly and unresponsive. They'd volunteered for poetry, it turned out, to escape from music. Their reaction, even to Hughes and Heaney, was groans and yawns. Asked to write a poem, they were sullen and mutinous.

Wednesdays were my teaching day. I got to dread them. It wasn't helped that I spent Tuesday nights tossing and turning or racked with nightmares. Part of the condition of my contract was to put together an anthology and organize a reading to which parents and governors would be invited. By the fifth and final week I was desperate. I'd got one day left to turn them on to poetry.

I'd prepared a session on poem portraits, using Norman MacCaig's poem 'Aunt Julia' as inspiration. But as I was waiting for the first group to come in I flicked through *The Rattle Bag*, the Heaney-Hughes anthology. My eye fixed on Robert Frost's poem, '"Out, Out –"', about a boy who accidentally cuts off his hand with a circular saw. On an impulse, I read them that instead:

The buzz saw snarled and rattled in the yard ...

The room went quiet. I could hear the boys' breathing; my voice almost a whisper as I neared the end:

No one believed. They listened at his heart.
Little – less – nothing! – and that ended it.

One boy remembered a brother drowning; another a grand-father's story of losing his leg in the War. They were interested;

engaged; even prepared to talk about the way Frost used language; suspense; the senses. Then, I set them to write: about
an accident; or something terrible happening. They had to use
the senses, like Frost; and write, if possible from their own
experience.

Before, I'd had to squeeze poems out of them like juice out
of dry lemons: and those were mostly clichéd and dull. Now,
they wrote freely and with energy and imagination: poems
about car and boating accidents; about scaldings and falling
out of trees, about baby seals being clubbed; about torturing
a cat.

The poem had the same effect on every group. Then, in the
final session of the day, just as the boys were about to begin
reading their poems aloud, the Head of English walked in.

'Carry on,' he said, and sat at the back.

It would be untrue to say that every poem was wonderful.
But they all had sparks of energy. And some, like Frost's poem,
were powerful and moving and shocking. There was one about
a boy losing his eye in a fight after a football match; and one
about a party of schoolchildren buried under an avalanche;
and another about a family burned alive in a house fire.

After every poem there was applause. But the teacher didn't
clap.

'They were good, weren't they?' I said to him when the
boys had left the classroom.

He said nothing: not 'Yes,' or 'No'.

The anthology never materialized. The evening reading
with the parents and governors was cancelled.

After that experience, I stopped going into schools. I got a
full-time job teaching in a college. Strangely, I began to address
sex and violence as themes in my own work. There's nothing
like forbidding something to make it the topmost thing in your

mind. But I don't think it had anything to do with the teacher's embargo. It's more likely I learned the lesson from the boys: writing about something that really engages you.

'A children's writer should, ideally, be a dedicated semi-lunatic.'
Joan Aiken

Paul Bailey

Some years ago, I was invited to attend a Salon du Livre in
Bordeaux, along with Beryl Bainbridge, Tom Sharpe and a
children's writer who looked like a plump doll, spoke in a
squeaky voice and told everyone incessantly how much she
appreciated 'black men's willies'. One memorable Saturday
afternoon, the four of us went to lunch at a superb restaurant
on the outskirts of the city. The publicity director of Penguin
France and her assistant acted as hosts, even though I was the
only Penguin author present. Beryl, loath to eat 'foreign muck',
was given a large tomato salad while the rest of us feasted on
red mullet and lamb. It was a sunny day, so we sat at a table
in the exquisite garden drinking champagne, Sancerre and
Château Haut-Batailley. The two French women were regaled
with stories of the children's writer's black lover's sexual
expertise, including his habit of removing his false teeth prior
to intercourse, and as we were laughing Tom Sharpe observed
laconically, 'What is it with this crazy dame?'

Two hours later, flushed and happy, we returned to the

Salon, to take part in a joint event. The interviewer was a
nervous man who was seriously unacquainted with our books.
In desperation he asked us what we thought of each other's
work. 'What a stupid bloody question,' Tom replied. 'No com-
ment.' Beryl and I both said that we were too embarrassed to
answer, and the children's writer squeaked, 'I've only ever
read one book – *Winnie the Pooh* – and I never finished it.' We
then became aware of a commotion in the packed audience,
which contained many schoolchildren who were studying
English. A tall, gaunt man wearing a beret and smoking a
foul-smelling cigarette made his way to the front with many
an '*Excusez-moi*' and jumped on to the platform. He sat down
next to Beryl and announced, '*Je pense que les autres écrivains
sont*' – and here he paused before shouting 'fucking cunts'.
The parents of the children whisked them out of the tent on
the instant. The man in the beret now had his hand up Beryl's
skirt. '*Je t'adore*,' he repeated over and over, while Beryl wondered aloud why he was saying 'shut that door'.

The man turned out to be Robin Cook, alias Derek Ray-
mond, whose crime novels – *How the Dead Live* and *I was Dora
Suarez* – were extremely popular in France, where he had lived
for eighteen years. He was very drunk that day. Beryl firmly
removed his roving hand. He stood up and straight away fell
over. Someone took him out of the tent, but the event was
already at an end.

The day's madness wasn't finished. None of Beryl's books
was on display, but a young girl asked her to sign a copy of John
Steinbeck's *Of Mice and Men*. Beryl remarked that she hadn't
written the novel and that she wasn't a man, but the girl insisted
on acquiring her signature. And later that evening the children's
writer revealed that she called her toothless black lover 'Georgie
Porgie' when his denture was safe in its bedside glass.

'If fortune turns against you, even jelly breaks your tooth.'
Persian proverb

Matthew Sweeney

It's a dangerous thing to have too many esses in a poem. Or to have a tooth clean-up too close to a reading. Or to chew a toffee just before the reading starts – a toffee that turns out to suddenly have acquired a very hard nut, that is actually a crowned front tooth complete with mounting spike.

I was in Torhout, in Belgium, doing a few days' work in a high school. Before coming over I'd been involved in the judging of a school poetry competition, and part of the prize for the winners was an early dinner in a restaurant with me. Some prize, I thought, but I went willingly – I had some bits of advice to give the young people about their writing, and food in Belgium tended to be good.

It was a girl and a boy who came to join me; the girl slim, diminutive, very confident, the boy, the first prize-winner, a bit on the shy side and fat. We chatted easily enough, they had pasta and coke, I had a rare chateaubriand, and red wine. When it came to the dessert we decided to skip it, but a plate with four toffees came gratis, and I unwrapped one of these and stuck it in my mouth as we walked out.

So I was in the snow when I extracted my tooth from the toffee and held it up. The cold wind whistled through the gap which the tip of my tongue instinctively went to fill. And I was on my way to the library where in five minutes I was expected to give a poetry reading.

Somewhere in the back of my mind I had a déjà vu about this happening once before, but long, long ago. All I remembered, though, was that it had been a toffee, too, that had done the damage on that occasion. I resolved there and then to give up toffees, but that wouldn't help me do the reading. As we picked our way carefully over the treacherous pavement, I chattered away, out of embarrassment, to the two young people. I knew that if they weren't with me they would be laughing their heads off. All my words were coming out lisped. And all those esses in my poems!

Out of desperation, and prompted by the branch of the memory that stays in the unconscious, I put my tooth up into the gap and tried to push it back in. After a few attempts I actually managed this. It stayed in! So I might be able to do the reading after all. Full of resolve, and ambition to give the best reading of the year, I hurried us along to the library.

The teacher who'd organized my visit was waiting for me with the librarian who would introduce me. He was a quiet, likeable and clearly very decent man. The librarian was a jolly, quite attractive blonde. She immediately handed me a copy of the poster for the event which had a title at the top, I noticed – *A Dramatic Whole*. Puzzled, I looked at this until the teacher laughed and said he'd taken it from one of my e-mails, and I remembered something about telling him a poetry reading was a dramatic event, albeit drama with a little d. He'd turned it into a big D. I smiled thinly and asked to see the reading space.

There were twenty or so chairs set up in what appeared to be the children's section of the library. As well as my reading, the presentation of the students' prizes would take place, and they would each read their winning poem. These had been nicely produced in a booklet. It was all very well organized. And the fact that the students would be there meant that their parents would be there also, so I would definitely have an audience.

I tried checking my e-mail but the computer I'd been shown to refused to co-operate, so I flicked through some magazines instead, seeing how much of the Flemish I could understand from my rusty German. People were drifting in. I went over and looked through the prizes I would be handing out to the students. I sat down at the table at the front and looked through the reading list I'd carefully prepared. I wasn't giving my tooth a thought.

When all the prizewinners had shown up it was decided that we should get going. The teacher told the audience about the competition, and how he'd coaxed me over to Torhout. I then gave a little spiel about poetry competitions, what I looked for, what I didn't want to see. The students came up one by one, received their prize from me, returned my smile, mumbled their poem and sat down. Their parents took photographs.

Then it was my turn. As I half-listened to the librarian introduce me, I was pumped up with adrenalin and raring to go. I got to my feet like a boxer coming out of his corner. I launched, without introduction, into the first poem. Two lines into the second, however, I felt the horrible sensation of my tooth loosening in my mouth. Sure enough, before I got to the end of the poem it was in my hand again and I was lisping the last lines. Most of the adults in the audience were sniggering. I shoved the tooth back up into my mouth and started on the third poem, but this rendition was altogether less confident, and involved constant flicks of the tongue to ensure the tooth was staying in place. Not satisfied with this, I kept bringing my right thumb up to push the tooth in. I must have looked like Charlie Chaplin in *The Great Dictator*. Not surprisingly, there were frequent unscheduled pauses in the delivery of the poem. Even the teenagers were laughing now. The librarian had to take herself outside, overcome with hilarity.

I glanced at my watch, and at my reading list. God, I wasn't even halfway through yet. This was the worst reading I'd ever do in my life. I asked the audience if any of them were dentists, but all I got were grinning shakes of head. I started on another poem, noticing with horror that it was the most s-ridden of them all. Halfway through the piece the tooth came flying out of my mouth and bounced on the floor, rolling under the feet of the fat boy who was in the front row. The momentum of the poem carried me on for a few lines toothless, lisping, until embarrassment made me stop. The audience was in stitches now. One of them cried out, 'I think it rolled over there!' Another shouted, 'There it is! Don't put your foot down! It's under your shoe!'

'Give me my tooth back,' I croaked, and watched as two squeamish girls recoiled from it, leaving the fat boy to pick it up and bring it to me, shaking his head.

This time I couldn't fix it in at all. The teacher was on his feet now, telling the audience that because of my dental problem the reading had to be abandoned. As the audience filed out, looking back at me, I was still struggling to get the tooth into my mouth.

'Abuse is often of service. There is nothing so dangerous to an author as silence.' Samuel Johnson

Chuck Palahniuk

My favourite signing story is about Stephen King, who one time signed books in Seattle until his fingers cracked and started to bleed. The publicist who watched this says how she had to hold an ice pack to King's shoulder the whole time, and the moment he asked for a bandage, a fan in line shouted for some of the blood. At that, all the fans shouted for some of Stephen King's blood on their books. The bandage never arrived, and after hours of bleeding, King left the event pale and flanked by bodyguards.

My point is, I always thought: 'What a pussy . . .'

On tour for my book, *Lullaby*, in September 2002 I had to rethink all that. In Chicago, while I signed books, mobbed for five hours, a young black man stood in my face and shouted, 'Every generation has to have its Dolph Lundgren . . . !'

In Austin, Texas, where they give out free beer while you sign, I did my job while a woman stood a foot away from me, asking the bookstore staff, 'Why should I wait in this long line to get my books signed by *that dickwad*?'

In Phoenix, a stunning transgender woman handed out Vic-odins in the crowd. Her name was Margo, but her friends called her 'the Margo Monster'. She heckled – which was fine and cool – until the college guys around her started yelling for the '. . . fucking bitch to fucking shut the fuck up'.

In Ann Arbor, Michigan, where people slept outside the bookstore to get good seats, I signed books for hours while someone trashed my room at the Sheraton, throwing food all over the bed.

In Washington DC, an angry woman pounded the outside of the store windows. She and her sons couldn't get inside because of over-crowding. Halfway through the signing, the manager leaned close to say the woman had called the fire marshal for revenge. At that, the police shut down the store.

In Boston, a small mob of people chased the car while my escort drove backwards down an alley, trying to escape. The whole time, as people banged on the car roof with their hands, the escort kept saying, 'This never happens with John Grisham . . .'

But in San Francisco . . .

I'd drunk two Red Bulls and swallowed four Advil, and still I could barely hold a pen. The room was packed with people, everyone sweating in the heat. As the event started, even more people forced their way in. Dressed as waiters, they each had a towel folded over one arm. They each had black eyes, bruised cheeks and split lips. As I started to read, they started throwing dinner rolls at each other. The store assumed I'd hired them for extra drama. I thought the store had.

The first ten minutes, I didn't acknowledge them because I thought I might be hallucinating from the Advil and Red Bull. Then a waiter vomited clam chowder down the front of the lectern. It was the local Cacophony Society, God bless them.

In Providence, Rhode Island, the bookstore manager put a bag of frozen peas on my shoulder, and it felt like heaven.

At that, Mr Stephen King, I apologize.

'Competitions are for horses, not artists.' Béla Bartók

John Hartley Williams

Memoir Included in the Report to the Investigative Committee on Literary Crimes

The only possible attitude one can have to literary prizes is that they are worthless appendages, gratifying to collect should one be lucky, not to be confused with literary merit but thank you, anyway, and this is the number of the appropriate bank account. I, Viktor Blobchinsky, contemplated the fact that my name had appeared on the shortlist for the O. Telsit prize, therefore, with considerable scepticism. It would be nice to have a weekend in Moscow. It would be good to get out of Omsk, where it was currently minus thirty-five degrees. Perhaps Peta Citanje, the birdwatching poetess, would be there. She too was a candidate. It later transpired she had prudently absented herself to Turkmenistan.

Following detailed instructions, I took a plane to our traffic-befouled capital, and turned up to read ten minutes'

worth of poems at the Ada Emil Theatre in Gonlinsit, a suburb
of Moscow not otherwise recorded on maps. The reading
would take place on the first evening; on the second evening
the prize would be awarded in the grand salon of the New
Kremlin Library. Usually I looked forward to meeting my
fellow poets, exchanging the time of day, telephone numbers,
gossip. It was not quite like that, this time. A Damoclean sword
hung over the proceeding, well illuminated, in the form of a
blue *toile*, with the legend 'O.Telsit Prize' upon it in yellow
cursive, and a fuzzy photo of the great Oskar himself, his beaky
visage peering down at posterity. No doubt he disapproved of
us. But there we were anyway, gathered round each other like
dogs in the park, exhibiting classic symptoms of cordiality and
paranoia: *the poets*. I recalled my peasant mother's dictum:
always show grace under fire my son. In fact, the word that kept
pounding through my brain was *run*.

Libra Cernow, the organizer, instructed me on the importance of timekeeping. *'Ten minutes only, Blobbo'* she instructed
me, Although I do not mind the driver of the number 29 tram
calling me Blobbo, I resent this affectionate soubriquet being
used by an apparatchik of the Committee of Letters. There
was no room in the tight schedule, however, for protest. There
were ten of us altogether. One hundred minutes of quivering
poetry voices. I slurped down some of the Red Dragon (a
fiery, Georgian wine) served in the bar of the Ada Emil and
wondered whether it had not been laced with some homicide-
inducing substance. I was itching to slip round the corner to
buy an axe. Certainly I was not anxious to perform.

Inside the theatre, we discovered the readings were to take
place on the stage set of the Nikolai Gogol play *Dead Souls*,
currently in production at the Ada Emil Theatre. This stage
set resembled an exploded diagram of a Russian log house,

its floorplanks sagging, its tables leaning, and all around it, rearing brokenly up at the edges, black sharks' teeth, as if a gargantuan mouth were about to swallow the entire construction. An alarming tilt had been applied to the stage floor, so that walking on it one felt one was on the deck of a ship that was about to capsize. One by one, my colleagues skipped or tripped (one actually fell) across the skewed living-room stage to a microphone that refused to be lowered or raised, and read their poems. A reverse alphabetical order of performance had been dictated by the Central Committee, so that I, Blobchinsky, would have to wait ninety nail-biting, Red-Dragon-swilling minutes before my turn would come. Peta Citanje being absent, her work was read by Janos Inkslane, a Hungarian hack from the Writer's Association. Inkslane reminded me of Hlestakov the trickster, a character in another play by Gogol. With limelight-hogging indifference to the plight of those who were waiting to follow him, he over-confidently overran. One hundred and twenty minutes. One hundred and thirty. I kept revising my appearance back. Conscious of the silent auditorium behind me, I began to speculate that the listless, capacity crowd was in fact constituted of unemployed actors who had failed to get a part in the current production of *Dead Souls*. They should not have failed. It was a superb performance.

When reading poems to an audience, I like to keep eye-contact with it, notice when it has fallen asleep or has started to do the *Pravda* crossword (even help it in that enterprise should the size of the public be sufficiently small to justify such interactivity – as is often the case). Tottering across the alarming stage to the microphone, however, I suspected the entire house had succumbed to slumber. The house lights were dimmed, and a blinding spot was trained on my face, so I could not confirm this. The combination of Red Dragon and stage-tilt were also ruinous to my composure. But I carefully placed my open fob-watch on the lectern. The exactness of my timekeeping would be a reprimand to the self-indulgent. At the very least my performance would wake people in time for the last tram back to town. But who were they, that invisible audience? Could it be that, asphyxiated in their seats in lifeless simulacrums of the poetry-loving, they were merely paid extras? Could it be the Committee of Letters had engaged them to convince foreign journalists Russian literature was alive and well? To convince *us* Russian literature was alive and well?

I took a deep breath, and began to recite the interesting lines that Gogol had written for my presentation. No, no, no! Where were my own poems? I riffled through the little pile of books in the hope of finding a poem that had been written by me. Once or twice I found something that bore a resemblance to a poem I had perhaps composed in my own person. Quite often, the poems seemed to be the interior monologue of a character called, in the Irish fashion, himself. What a subtly drawn portrait that was! Not only was this Blobchinsky full of fraud, guile, melancholy, Red Dragon, and unreasonable hope, he was also a grotesque nullity who brought tears of laughter into the eyes of the speechless audience. When the insincere applause came, he staggered off. Blobchinsky, the poet. A man who had simply renounced poetry. Who had written it and then denounced it and then denounced himself and been shot. Taken out and lined up against the wall of the Ada Emil Theatre and shot. Bang. Not a tragic character. By this time the audience was recovering its departed spirits. How rarely did it get to see a one hundred per cent holy Russian fool?

On the Monday following these dismal histrionics, I spent the morning in bed. From the copy of *Pravda* which had slithered under my hotel room door, I began to fashion little pipe people. I then drew simulacrums of the faces of the Telsit Prize judges on each one and placed them in my cloak. I now had the judges, Beria, Malenkov, Krill and Arsine Bone – all of them – in my pocket. Ho ho ho. At noon, I raised myself up, walked to a local ironmonger's and bought a short-handled axe. Then I returned to my hotel room. The telephone was ringing. What could that be? Notification that I had in fact won and would be awarded the prize that evening? Trembling, I picked up the receiver and heard the distant voice of Plumpchov assuring me that my book *Nicaragua* was certain to carry off the laurels. I put down the receiver. The phone rang again. It was Dobrilovic. My book *Argentina* was sure to win. Just his little joke. But I, Blobbo, had been in the system long enough to know when I was being set up. Had I not, myself, sent thousands of innocents to an early grave? Well, no, actually. Although it felt like it. More phone calls. Half the Committee of Letters. Their egregious friendliness finally managed to dupe me, sweetly bolstering my self-esteem. Should I leave the axe behind? I was halfway down the grubbily-carpeted stairs when I changed my mind, went back, and secreted it in my sleeve.

The New Kremlin Library's grand entrance might have been designed as a reproach to the meekness of poetry. I was late. A frosty Libra Cernow attempted to get me to deposit my bearskin hat, my thick sheepskin cloak, with the cloakroom girls. The press were waiting to take everybody's photograph. Well, why did they not simply wait to photograph the winner when he, or she, had won? Why such a display of inclusiveness, when the mechanism was designed to propel us forcibly out of the entrance we had just been ostensibly welcomed in by? I refused. The beaming attendant who took my invitation card recoiled gratifyingly from proximity to my cloak.

I returned his beam. He led me to a concourse alive with the
drone of talent-assassinating gossip, and I stood for a moment
contemplating the vivacious body language of the assembly.
It suggested lustful participation at a mass hanging. My photograph was taken. A battery of flashes exploded. Did they have
film in their cameras? I hailed many people by their wrong
name. Waiters who found the quickest way to offload their
little trays was to cruise in my vicinity ferried me glass upon
glass of *Skrimskaia*. This was a very different crowd from the
night before: literary editors, cultural bureaucrats, publishers,
critics – people who would not be seen dead at a mere poetry
reading.

Executions were another matter.

I looked around at my fellow-poets. It was pitiful. I could
see by their glowing faces that they thought they had got away
with something, that they had pulled something off. One look
at the Central Committee should have told them otherwise.
The moment came. Angelica Krill, the bulky Chairman of the
Judges, rose to her feet and began to read out assessments of
the candidates' books. Her speech developed horrid momentum. Every warm sentiment contained a barb, each laudatio a
dagger. I watched the apprehensive faces of my fellow literati,
ignominious mugs that we all were, with a mixture of hostility,
contempt and pity. For myself, I reserved those same emotions
– only twice times over. Krill was reading out the list of names
of the candidates as if they were signed confessions. We had
simply lined ourselves up, had we not? We had wept and
testified that yes, yes we wanted to be hanged, now please.
We had imputed all manner of disgusting literary crimes to
ourselves. I learned from the prune-like lips of Krill that my
own writing 'taught us what it feels like to be a man' – slander-
ous balderdash, if ever I'd heard it. The roll call was complete,

all the names had been read out, only one name had not had a reservation attached to it. I could see the lugubrious Arsine Bone smirking. Of course! His protégé! The well-known name of the short Kazakhstan informer was pronounced the winner, a man who had plea-bargained himself into freedom and sacrificed everyone of his comrades as he did so. As soon as the extent of this treachery became apparent to me, I felt I was falling, and the New Kremlin Library was really a vast literary mauseoleum into which poets like myself would forever be poured and concreted over whilst a small orchestra played patriotic music, flashbulbs popped and *Skrimskaia* was swigged by the cheerful.

When the applause faded, I downed an entire bottle in front of an astonished waiter, scurried off to a telephone kiosk, pulled out the small effigies of the jury I had made and hacked them to pieces with the axe, uttering small cries and dribbles. Then I strode keening through the New Kremlin Library, scattering a paper trail of betrayal and indignity. I freely admit that in my heart I wished to commit a crime that would reverberate down the centuries. I could not, however, think of one dreadful enough and so I rushed off to find a taxi to bear myself incognito from that dreadful spot, hating myself, loathing the whole detestable show, admitting to myself that, yes, I had compromised myself utterly by submitting to the whole disgusting charade, all because some public relations shark had decided it was good for publicity and *may a dog fuck his mother and the mother of the central committee.* I had done what I'd always sworn I'd never do (and would never do again); I should have stood defiantly on that stage, thrown my book at the audience, blown my nose on my beard, unzipped my fly, wee-weed over my fellow poets where they sat dumbly staring up at me, shouted *Long Live the Revolution!* and then gone home for pickled herrings and a glass of milk and allowed the thrilling glow of pure civil disobedience to resume uninterrupted usurpation of my heart.

V. Blobchinsky (poet)

'It was wonderful to find America, but it would have been more wonderful to miss it.' Mark Twain

Margaret Drabble

The lowest moment in my literary career was when I found myself bidding for a middle-aged oil magnate in a mock slave auction at a dinner in Dallas. I was bidding for the sake of Bloomsbury and for the honour of England, but I think that compounds the shame. I don't often look back at that evening. It is all a bit of a blur.

I can't even remember what year it was. It must have been after Michael and I were married, because it was largely his fault. In marrying Michael, I married into Bloomsbury. I had long enjoyed a vexed and sometimes tearful relationship with Virginia Woolf, who would have despised me as much as I admire her, but I had not taken on board all her family, friends and associates, nor had I ever expected to find myself in Texas on a fund-raising trip for the conservation of Charleston Farmhouse in Sussex. I was anxious in advance. Like Thoreau (or was it Emerson?) I distrust all enterprises that require new clothes, and this trip strongly suggested that I needed additions to my wardrobe. I consulted a friend familiar with the soap opera named *Dallas*, who told me I needed a cocktail dress and a hairstyle. I have never had a hairstyle. I went to a hairdresser and asked for one, but he didn't seem able to help. I've got the wrong kind of hair for a hairstyle.

The trip had its good moments, and we travelled in good company. The tall, slender and ever-charming Duke of Devonshire was one of the party: he would rise gracefully to his feet on any occasion and declare that this was the happiest and proudest moment of his life. The diminutive Hugh Casson was equally suave and equally appealing. Michael and I did our best, in our own fashion, delivering respectable lectures in aid of the good cause. Mine was on Mr Bennett and Mrs Woolf, in which I daringly suggested that Arnold Bennett and Virgina Woolf had more in common than was usually recognized. We also appeared with Lynn Redgrave in a performance of Virginia Woolf's not very entertaining home entertainment, *Freshwater*. But despite these eccentric efforts to enlist the support of the rich art-lovers of Texas, the walls of whose ranches were hung with works by Monet and Degas, we failed to open their purses for Charleston. The price of oil was at that time very low – I think it had fallen to eight dollars a barrel – and the Prince of Wales had been in Dallas just before us begging on behalf of some other British charity. He had mopped up whatever spare cash they had, and there was nothing left for us.

All hung on the success of the final Gala Dinner and Auction, which was held in the newly-opened Versailles-style hotel in which we were all lavishly accommodated. The actor Robert Hardy was to play auctioneer for us. We dressed up as best we could, and descended to meet the wealthy guests, one of whom bore the familiar name of Ellen Terry. She was small and plump and in real estate. She glittered tremendously in a splendid ball gown. I felt quite shy in my modest Monsoon silk. We drank a cocktail or two, and mingled. We went on and on mingling. Something had gone wrong with the catering, and the dinner was seriously delayed. The Texans, angered already by the oil slump, were not amused. By the time we staggered to our tables, we were all completely drunk, and the guests were turning nasty.

Poor Robert Hardy had the task of trying to sell various bejewelled trinkets that had been donated to the appeal. These were mere trifles, worth only a few thousand dollars apiece, and the Texans despised them. They refused to bid. In vain did he urge them on with many blandishments: the old English charm had ceased to work. I can't remember how the suggestion of a slave auction arose – certainly not from our Bloomsbury party. A tanned, gold-bangled JR look-alike offered himself as a prize, but again, nobody bid. In the end, urged on by fellow diners at our table, I boldly opened the bidding. I can't remember what I offered for him, nor can I recollect what happened next. Somebody must have outbid me, for at least I didn't have to claim him. Or if I did, I soon lost him, because I certainly haven't got him now.

How did the evening end? How did we manage to put ourselves to bed? We both woke with spectacular hangovers, worthy of Lucky Jim himself, and I had the added shame of knowing that I had been a disgrace to Bloomsbury, and had given Virginia Woolf yet more reasons to despise me. What vulgarity, what immodesty! I am left with a lingering sense of horror, and a feeling that I had wandered into the wrong kind of novel. And it wasn't even the kind of novel that I could write. But will I ever learn to stay at home? Well, I hope not. It will all come in handy one day, surely.

'My Oberon! What visions have I seen!
Methought I was enamoured of an ass.'
Shakespeare, *A Midsummer Night's Dream*

Colm Tóibín

I had published my first novel. It was called *The South*. I was on my first tour and this was Boston. The schedule said I was to do a TV show, and thus I found myself, make-up on, ready to appear, sitting in a room waiting to be called into the studio. The show was live, and when I looked at the screen I saw that Norman Mailer was already on the programme.

'That is Norman Mailer!' I said to the two women in the room. 'That's amazing!'

I don't remember how I realized that one of the people to whom I was gushing was Mrs Mailer. She was very beautiful and very cool. Her skin was perfect. She stared at the screen, expressionless.

'Am I on after him?' I asked the production assistant.

'Yeah, you're on after him,' the production assistant said.

I smiled at Mrs Mailer as if to say that we were in this together, but she remained placidly staring at her husband as he spoke, his wonderful worn face in full flight on the screen, his arms gesticulating.

Time went on. We continued to watch in silence. I knew the show was twenty-nine minutes long. Mailer was still on *The Deer Park* after fifteen. Then he talked about Marilyn and the Kennedys. He smiled, he laughed, he shrugged his shoulders, he interrupted the questions. At twenty-five, he was discussing *The Executioner's Song*.

'Don't worry,' the production assistant said to me, 'keep calm. It'll soon be your turn.'

At twenty-seven and a half minutes, they rushed me past Norman Mailer and put me sitting in his chair and miked me while the camera focused on the host holding up a copy of Mailer's new book.

The chair where Mailer had been sitting was still warm. I thought about Mailer's ass, I imagined it short and muscular and strong, hairy but not fleshy, the grey hair darkening towards the deep cleft. The heat from his ass was going through me as I said a few words about my book and then the show came to an end before the heat had faded.

Mailer was outside putting on his coat. I placed my book down on the table while I reached for my bag. He looked at the book. I wondered if I could start to tell him how much I admired his work, how the sweeping, fiery tones of *The Armies of the Night* and *Miami and the Siege of Chicago* had made me want to be a journalist, but how I believed that *The Executioner's Song* was a masterpiece, as good as it gets, how that book made me want to do nothing except read it again.

'You're Irish,' he said and took me in with his clear gaze.

I nodded. He studied the book again. I wondered if he was going to ask me if he could have a copy of it. I wondered if I should offer him one. It had taken me years to write.

'The Outh,' he said, approvingly, touching the jacket of the book.

'No,' I said almost breathlessly, *'The South.'*

He seemed puzzled. We both looked down at the jacket.

The graphic designer had made a beautiful 'S' in a different colour and type-face to the 'O-u-t-h' so that the last four letters were perfectly clear against a blue background, but the 'S' was not so clear. I traced my finger along the 'S' to show him it was there. He smiled sadly.

'So it's not *The Outh*?' His tone was amused, relaxed, mellow. He seemed to have liked saying the word 'Outh', he had made it long and glamorous-sounding and the afterglow of saying it stayed with him now in a slow smile.

He began to turn. His wife was waiting for him.

'I thought it was an Irish word,' he said.

Then he gathered himself up and left. I glanced sharply at his ass as he moved towards the door. It was everything I thought it might be and more. And then he was gone.

'There still remains, to mortify a wit,
The many-headed monster of the pit.'
Pope, *Epilogue to the Satires*

Louise Welsh

Some people have a taste for humiliation. When I worked as
a secondhand dealer there was a collector of tawse[1] who was
famous around the markets. He excused his obsession by
explaining he was planning to open a school museum. We
suspected instead a rare Scottish strain of 'the English disease'.[2]
Humiliation was undoubtedly his kink and he worked hard
for it. It saddens me that this man had to trawl car boot sales
and secondhand shops in search of humiliation, while I experience it so frequently and with so little effort.

Describing the beautiful romance between Robert Louis
Stevenson and his wife Fanny Osborne, I told a lecture theatre
of young students, 'Stevenson went across the Atlantic in
search of Fanny.' The hilarity stretched all the way to Sil-

---

[1] Leather belt until fairly recently used by Scottish teachers to ritually
humiliate children by strapping them across their hands in front of
the rest of the class/school.
[2] Spanking.

verado. At least that got a laugh. Unlike when (I'm cringing as I write this) I asked a member of my visually impaired writer's workshop about the lack of description in his writing and he reminded me he'd been blind from birth.

Some humiliations feel like triumphs. Initially flattered to be hailed by a hard-drinking young literary lion in a hotel corridor, I started to wonder why he was telling me of the mess he had made of his bathroom. Was this monologue on his lack of aim some kind of metaphor? Then it dawned. He thought I was a cleaner and was instructing me to erase his jottings. Keeping in character I told him he was too old to expect anyone to mop up his toileting accidents and to do it himself or I'd phone the *TLS*.

Masochists note, an audience salts any wound. I enjoy readings. I prepare and don't feel that nervous. It's my body that lets me down, hands that tremble too much to lift a glass and, occasionally, a shaking leg which must have the audience wondering why the woman on stage is doing an impersonation of Elvis Presley. I remind myself the audience have paid good money to attend. They wish me well. This is a foolish delusion. At an Edinburgh Festival event entitled *Provocations* the first question came from an elderly woman. She looked handknitted, but was about as woolly as a Rottweiler. In polite shortbread tones she began by recounting avant-garde writers she admired, including Burroughs and Trocchi. Surprised but delighted, the readers on stage cast coy glances at each other. Then she got to the meat of her statement.

'I would like to know why this event is called *Provocations*? I've been sitting here all morning and I haven't been provoked once! No,' her voice rose, 'nothing I've heard this morning has provoked me.' Her friend patted the woman's arm soothingly. But the old lady would not be pacified. 'I came here expecting to be provoked,' the voice reached a pitch dogs find uncomfortable, 'and I have been sorely disappointed!'

Later I asked my sister what we had looked like sitting on the platform before the unprovoked woman's tirade.

'You know,' she said thoughtfully, 'you looked like a group of West Coast councillors being quizzed about their expenses.'

What could be more humiliating?

'One place is everywhere, everywhere is nowhere.' Persian proverb

Mark Doty

I haven't even finished reading the letter of invitation to the Aran Islands Poetry Festival and I'm daydreaming of lonely sheep scrambling over the stones, and the wind blowing a salty mist over Inisboffin. Men in thick cable sweaters and thicker brogues. Hot whiskey with lemon on a raw night. Seals watching from the rocky shore. Will I come for airfare and enough money to buy dinner in Dublin? You bet.

I don't pay too much attention to the disclaimer that the conference actually takes place in Galway City, but the reality of this hits home the morning our taxi enters the driveway of the 'Hospitality Village', a compound on the edge of the university. A sprawl of concrete dorms, some bushes planted here and there, a flat brown building full of vending machines – it looks like an apartment complex in either Iowa City or Bratislava. We're given a key and a map, and wander our way around dozens of identical compounds to find OUR compound. By now we've decided it's an apartment complex on the outskirts of Prague. Our room seems meant to standardize life for the struggling classes. Two beds, each wearing a grey-striped mattress thin as an overcoat, are bolted to the walls; overhead, a sizzle of fluorescent bulbs makes the whole place vibrate. Nothing anywhere indicates anything about the possibility of heat.

Well, what matter a spartan accommodation? We're off to find the conference. The path winds beside the dorms, beside a somewhat scruffy meadow and a dour stream, underneath what must surely be the only freeway in Western Ireland, past various discarded appliances rusting in the grass, nearly loses itself in some parking lots, and after a mile gives reluctantly onto the campus. A good bit of wandering and some puzzling campus maps lead us to the information table, where we're face to face with Mary-Grace, the travel agent who's put all this together. A line of senior citizens with rather strained expressions waits to talk to her, but nothing in her face betrays the least bit of stress. In fact, her dome of blonde hair seems as if it might serve as a kind of protective shield, repelling all difficulties. She waves the troubled participants aside to hand us name tags and a packet of information, and point out where to get something to eat.

Indeed we're starving, especially after more map consultation and wandering to find the school cafeteria. Eventually a pair of unmarked swinging doors lead us into a basement chamber from which – were there justice in this world – we'd have heard the cries of the damned arising. For indeed the school cafeteria turns out to be half-Dante, half-Dickens. The staff has been recruited from a nineteenth-century orphanage. They stand, pale and defiant with gloom, behind trays of foods relentlessly brown and grey: porridges, gruel, sad toasted things, sorry boiled items, heartbroken sausages swimming in grey juice. We are too hungry to turn back, and choose what we think we can abide, and carry our trays to the towering, pale cashier – in her grey uniform she's either a moonlighting prison guard or a recently deinstitutionalized patient recovering from electroshock. At our table we translate the alarming bill from pounds and realize we've just spent twenty-five dollars on a breakfast that seems to be made of boiled, chilled elastic stockings.

Now despite these complaints, I am not particularly fussy about my circumstances. I have a friend, for instance, a well-known poet who is famous for refusing the rooms he is offered by well-meaning sponsors, referring to himself in the third person and declaring, '— does not sleep here!' I have never done this, though here in the infernal cafeteria I begin to think I should. I have been too grateful to be asked; I have been so surprised and pleased that people wanted to hear my work, or ask me what I thought, that I've said yes too easily. This phase of my life seems to be ending, even as I fail to finish my breakfast.

A quick conference with our fellow conferees reveals that the only other food to be had is in Galway City, a walk of another mile or more. We set off, passing Mary-Grace at her table where a longer line of participants with problems wait to enlist her help. We note that all the clientele seem to be elderly, all rather alike in their appearance, and a bit familiar – of course, they're Boston Irish! Here for a vacation on the old sod with a bit of literature thrown in. My writerly colleagues and I are the lure to get them to plunk down their dollars for a vacation at Hospitality Village – but wait, where are my fellow writers? Wiser than me, clearly, or maybe they read the fine print; they appear for their readings and promptly vanish into rental cars, gone into the rain. Said rain now slicks the path to Galway City and then the way home, and then the path. Rainwater cascades down from the freeway; truck tyres throw out gritty spray, and there's nothing to do but make a run through it.

I will skip the increasingly long lines shadowing Mary-Grace, and the anguished pleas spoken into the pay-phone outside our door, and go right to the outing which lent the festival its name. A couple of hundred participants, so much white hair among us that altogether we call up something of those fine Aran sheep I imagined so long ago, are herded onto buses, and from the buses to a ferry, and across the chilly sound toward the fabled islands. The air's exuding something heavier than mist but lighter than rain. We huddle inside the unheated big cabin of the ferry, where you can buy coffee and tea and buns.

Lucky those who do! Since once we arrive at Inishmore, there is no food to be had. The reception organized to greet us turns out to be a tiny, rather pleasing band, playing a pair of welcoming tunes. We listen politely, though it is a bit chilly to be standing here by the dock in the more-than-mist. Once they're through we begin our march in the now only slightly-less-than-rain. Our destination: a ring fort, an ancient site on a high spot from whence one could indeed see much of the world, were there any world today to be seen. The path wends on, past stones and the requisite, rather glum sheep. Soon the path is going over the stones, since of course the pastures are divided by stone walls just tall enough to keep those wandering clouds in place. At each of these hurdles we lose at least one or two of our company: 'Oh, I think I'll just sit this out,' or 'I'll wait here, Helen, you go on and don't worry about me.' It'll be a long wait.

It is quite a hike to the ring fort still, and among our troupe a restless apprehension has begun to spread: we are too polite to say it at first, and surely someone has thought of this problem, but there don't seem to be any bathrooms. Did you happen to notice a bathroom? We would ask Mary-Grace but she seems to have stayed back at the ferry. Or did she vanish with the bus?

The best the sun can manage is a sort of coppery blush, and then it seems to give up entirely and things grow darker. Our band has diminished but we are still plenty, and we are committed; we want to see the ring fort at the summit of our journey, and we want to hear the reading promised there; Edna O'Brien herself will speak among the ancient stones.

And indeed, at the summit, to the wonder of a crowd now damp, hungry, and accepting that the shame of simply going and relieving oneself beside one of the stone walls is preferable to the misery of keeping one's pride intact, Edna O'Brien appears. How has she done it? She looks as though she has just returned from the powder room. She is radiant, untouched; she is funny, smart and wise; her tenderness toward the world is balanced by her unmistakable, perfectly pitched anger. We love her.

And then we walk down again.

The elderly Irish of Boston are sore, their stockings torn. They are faint with hunger and exposure, and mildly seasick. Thank heavens tomorrow's the day to go home. The buses will be late, and there won't be enough of them to get us all to Shannon on time. Paul and I are lucky to claim seats. Mary-Grace gets on the bus and makes an announcement that only those on early flights should take this bus. She asks Paul and I to get off and take a later bus. I do not have a shred of faith that there will BE a later bus, and I am finished with Mary-Grace. No more Mr Nice Guy poet; Doty does not sleep here! Mary-Grace, I say, with a steely ferocity in my voice which makes six rows of heads swivel, and which startles me, though I rather like it, we are riding on this bus.

And we do. We barely make the plane. We're not surprised to see, as we fit ourselves and our carry-ons into the tiny space of our coach seats, Mary-Grace looking back at us with a quick, evaluative glance, just before she disappears into First Class.

'We are more anxious to speak than to be heard.' Thoreau

Michael Ondaatje

I did hear this one true story – the nightmare event at a reading.

A well-known American novelist, after her successes, was invited back to her high school. They had put on the dog for her and she had therefore put on the dog for them. She dressed well and stood up at the lectern to give her formal speech about writing, the arts, culture, education – all the noble things writers never talk or think about when they are not on panels or speaking publicly.

It was a full auditorium. Halfway through the talk she began to feel sick and, knowing she was soon going to throw up, announced in a calm voice that she had left a few pages of her speech offstage, in her bag. She walked off slowly and as soon as she was out of sight ran to the bathroom and threw up noisily. She had been doing this for about a minute when someone came into the bathroom to tell her that the lapel mike was still on.

'He who is wrong fights against himself.' Egyptian proverb

James Wood

One of Lichtenberg's aphorisms goes: 'an erratum in the list of errata'. I've always liked this spindly joke, not only because the double negative is witty (might an erratum in the list of errata be not wrong but mysteriously right, as in algebra a minus times a minus equals a plus?) but because Lichtenberg seems to imply that error attracts more error; or rather that the urge to correction carries the seeds of its own destruction, as saintliness attracts martyrdom.

For those who make a living from writing, getting things wrong constitutes the formal, not to say canonical nightmare. To publicize error is to multiply it infinitely. And how much more acute is the embarrassment of error for one whose job, as a critic, is to correct others' fallacies? That error attracts more error I know to my cost. My first book, a collection of essays, contained a piece on Jane Austen. Though I knew perfectly well that Lady Catherine de Bourgh belongs to *Pride and Prejudice* and Lady Bertram to *Mansfield Park* – though who will now believe me? – I placed Lady Catherine de Bourgh in *Mansfield Park*. Stranger still, in the same paragraph, I misspelt that formidable lady's name (as de Burgh, like the near-singer Chris de Burgh) and wrote that throughout the novel she is more interested in her rug than in her children. Austen in fact wrote that she was more interested in her pug than in her children.

As far as I know, these were the only errors in my book; yet in one small paragraph, three howlers! (And how painful that word howler is when it is used not by you but against you in a review, conjuring flocks of correctors cawing at you in unison.) Two reviewers of the book noticed, and both, of course, rightly went to town on the information – went to town and had dinner at my expense. One of them suggested that such howlers – that word! – shook his confidence in the entire book.

Like most writers, and certainly most journalists, I work, and work most happily, from memory. Memory is organic. The notorious fact-checkers of the *New Yorker* are irritating not only because they often prove how fallible are our memories, but because they seem to mechanize what ought to be a natural, unmediated, fast-moving process. As a teenager I loved Ford Madox Ford's opinionated and breezy *The English Novel* (I still remember its sky-blue Carcanet paper cover) and found romantic Ford's preface, in which he says, or so I recall, that he wrote the book in six weeks on a becalmed ship, far from home and far from his books. Erich Auerbach famously wrote his great work *Mimesis* in Istanbul during the Second World War, again far from his books, and without access to libraries. Chesterton deliberately quoted, and certainly misquoted from memory at all times, on principle. This is surely the scholar's and writer's ideal, and I have a curious ritual, in which, if forced to look a quote up that I once knew by heart, I try to read it through, close the book, and put it into my piece using my lightly renewed memory. I did this when writing the Austen essay. I consulted *Mansfield Park* for the quote in which Austen writes that Lady Bertram was more interested in her pug than her children, closed the book, and then reproduced the quote from memory. In my mind, I had fixed Lady Bertram as perhaps doing needlework in her drawing room while her children came and went, or perhaps, like Emma Woodhouse's hypochondriacal father, fussing with a rug over her knees. I had utterly forgotten about the pug, as one does forget such things years after reading a novel. That I misremembered the pug is uninteresting; but that I made two other errors in the same paragraph seems to be a perfect example of my unconscious madly semaphoring to my conscious mind – 'stop, stop: you are in error and wading deeper with every step!'

But why do we all prefer to use our memories rather than look things up? The memory, after all, is an error-producing organ, as the police know only too well from millions of fallacious eyewitnesses. We do it not only because it is easier than trotting to the shelves, but to show off – not to others, who after all can't know we have used our memories unless we tell them so in print. We do it to show off to ourselves. But since using our memory is certainly bound to lead to error, the conclusion must be that showing off to ourselves is really – however unconsciously – commending ourselves for getting things wrong. Showing off to ourselves is getting things wrong to the secret satisfaction of our unconscious. And the further conclusion to be drawn from this is that we want to be caught at it. We want to be mortified. We want to be punished for being the kind of people who get things wrong; we want to be mortified for being the kind of people who show off to ourselves. Memory is vanity; all is vanity, saith the preacher. This is circular, you'll protest. Yet mortification is a religious notion at heart, and a great deal of Dostoevsky and Hamsun turns on precisely the idea that we really crave our own mortification. It was Augustine, the great religious theorist of error, who first proposed a real theory of memory. He suggested that we only remember things by having already forgotten them beforehand. Or at least I think he said this. I can see the passage, underlined, in my Penguin copy of his *Confessions*. But I am far from home, and writing this far from my books . . .

'Trouble will rain on those who are already wet.' Spanish proverb

Patrick McCabe

And so at last the big day had arrived and there I was with my bags and papers happily on board an Aer Lingus plane. En route to Scotland's magical capital, named after Edwin, king of ancient Northumbria, chiselled architectural master-piece of eras both Georgian and Victorian. For the purposes of refreshment on my journey, I sipped some tea and treated myself to a pastry and a snippet or two of Bertrand Russell. I could not believe my eyes when, a mere forty minutes later, I looked out the window and perceived not, as I had expected, a tranquil stretch of snotgreen ocean, but a magnificent castle dramatically perched on a precipitous crag of volcanic rock!

Within the hour I had arrived in my bedroom, thoroughly debagged and ironing with an application that can only be described as 'furious'.

'If there's a trouser press in the hotel, you make sure and use it!' I recalled my wife's admonition. And now, here I was, with that very implement to hand!

I was in the process of climbing into my perfectly configured strides when, quite unexpectedly, the air was sharply rent by the piercing sound of a phone. I clambered across the floor and tore at the recalcitrant receiver. I pressed it to my ear and heard the animated tones of my agent. 'Not long to go now!' he exclaimed. 'Are you nervous, Pat? Or should I say – author of *Carn*? Ha ha!'

Some time later, inexplicably, I found myself quite nervous so I decided the best thing to do was to avail myself of some exercise. I ran around the hotel a number of times, then retired to the bar for some drinks. After seven or eight brandies I found myself ready to face my public.

The sight that greeted us in Charlotte Square was truly astonishing. The first thing was – the actual *size* of the tent.

'*Good evening Edinburgh!*' I heard myself barking in the – as yet, quite empty, marquee – '*Hope y'all feeling good tonight!*'

'Lady!' I declared to the woman who approached us, on the verge of giving her the soul-bro 'handclasp' (I had read about Allen Ginsberg doing that with 'the Beats').

She smiled faintly – then, to my amazement, walked right past! 'I'm afraid there's been a misunderstanding,' I heard her say, 'your client's not reading here. Harold Pinter is.'

'Harold Pinter?' my agent replied.

'Yes. He's my favourite writer,' she said. 'Oh! The Caretaker!'

I was close to fainting.

Somewhere to the north, I heard a clap of thunder rolling broodily behind the clouds. Just then, another official arrived on the scene – sporting a name badge reading MADGE – wondering aloud if it could be possible I was reading in '*Winnie's place*'?

It was just at that moment that the heavens, as earlier celestial disgruntlements had indicated they might, decided to open up once and for all, mercilessly lashing the tent with bullwhips.

Once outside, my agent brightened and slapped me blowsily on the back.

'Don't worry, Pat! You'll do the reading of a lifetime and then it'll back with the pair of us to the comfort of the festival club!'

'That's the spirit!' chimed Madge, before waving goodbye and ducking back inside, pausing only to chuck away the remainder of the mutant-like grey sludge that had once been the festival programme.

We prayed the pulverizing skies would relent, fortifying ourselves with dreamlike exchanges regarding the 'bottle of champagne' that my agent pledged he would purchase whenever our 'travails' had concluded.

Its 'bubbling sparks' to be sweeter than any 'ice-cold' – in 'Alex' or anywhere else.

We were received by yet another elegantly-attired lady – this time bearing a name badge reading WINNIE.

'Such a downpour!' she groaned, before adding: 'We're ready to start at nine, Mr Maccabbee.'

'Moët & Chandon,' whispered my agent as we followed our host inside. 'Just think of it.'

Winnie smiled and craned her neck around the door to see was there anyone coming. There wasn't. I walked around for a bit, inspecting the books. It was a nice library and very well kept – that has to be acknowledged.

Leafing through what I think was a crime novel of some description, I was quite taken aback to hear the sound of someone roaring and then glass smashing just directly outside. I looked up to see a wild-eyed *clochard* launching *sorties* in the direction of the door, hurling himself at it and waving a jagged-edged bottle, discharging as he did so what can only be described as an 'endless stream of incomprehensible phonetic-based gibberish'.

'That's Timmy,' Winnie fumed, securely bolting the door, adding: 'It's just not good enough! He steals books and sells them for money! He thinks we don't know – but we do, don't we, Moira?'

'Oh yes!' returned Moira. 'Four *Just William*s he removed last week! But that's the end of it! That's the end of it now! We've been far too tolerant! Far too tolerant, Mr McCabbee!'

'Ha ha!' I found myself on the verge of ejaculating. 'For a minute there I was sure he was a fan!'

'Hmm!' she mused, inspecting her watch. 'Speaking of which – it's getting late!'

Just then there was a knock at the door.

'Don't open it!' cautioned Winnie. 'It might be Timmy!'

'No, he's gone, thank heavens!' her colleague replied. 'Didn't you hear him kicking the allotment bins?'

'Of course!' replied Winnie.

The doors were promptly unbolted and we surmised the status of this new arrival.

'Ah for the love of God – how are ye all doin'?' She beamed and it was then I noted her carrier bags, containing – *mirabile dictu!* – a hardback copy of *The Essential James Joyce!*

It was the moment I had been waiting for. 'Aha, so!' I heard myself saying. 'A countrywoman of my own perchance?'

'Could ye direct me to Charlotte Square please? I have to go to a reading,' she told us.

Our visitor was led towards the door as, crestfallen, I watched her eagerly accept directions in dumbshow. How salutary and invigorating it would be to declare that at that very second, against all the odds, my agent and I looked up to descry hordes of novel-wielding writers bearing down upon us, exhausted, but unmistakably revivified on seeing us as they wept: *'Please tell us that the Patrick McCabe reading hasn't started yet!'*

It was never destined to happen. What was, however, was that the allotment bins were to receive another kicking as we looked up to see Timmy waving his fist and bawling: 'I'll get you, Auld Sticky-Knickers! You'll no' chase me!'

'Now now!' croaked Winnie. 'That's no attitude!' as the philistine derelict took his leave once more. Before – *deus ex machina* – I felt my elbow being tugged and, to my delight, found myself being addressed by the most refined and aristocratic of ladies – also, I noted, the bearer of some literature, although this time of the 'magazine' variety.

'Is it alright if I – ?' I heard her say.

'By all means!' I yelped, and bundled her inside.

With pounding heart, I took my position upon the podium, gingerly opening my book and launching into a potted history of my novel, explaining briefly how it had come into being and why I'd decided to be a writer. Warming to my subject, I heard tumultuous cheers. Base as it was, I could not dispel the notion that at that very moment Harold Pinter was making good his escape, falling across Charlotte Square as whoops of derisive laughter chased him all down Princes Street, followed by jeers of: 'Pauses, Harold? We don't need no steenking pauses! It's *Carn* we're after, pal – *comprende*?'

Despite everything that had happened, somehow at last it all seemed worth it. I lowered my head, in a gesture of 'unworthiness' and abject humility. Then, with a cough, I proceeded. 'I'd like to read you an extract,' I said, raising my eyes after some considerable length of time to witness, to my horror, my entire audience making for the door.

'No! Don't go!' I called. 'I'm not finished yet!'

She stood and looked at me for a minute then aggressively retorted: 'I have better things to do than listen to this. I just came in out of the rain!' before disappearing forever.

We waited, hopelessly, for another ten minutes, and then at last I heard Winnie say: 'I simply can't understand it. We sent out leaflets to *all* the housing schemes!'

'Perhaps we should call it a day,' my agent ventured hesitatingly, before adding: 'After all, we have an important engagement, haven't we, Patrick?'

'Ice-cold in Eddie!' I responded grittily. 'With Moët & Chandon.'

Which indeed we had – and, boy, were we going to enjoy those bubbles as they cheekily burst on our tongues!

Once more finding ourselves swinging into Princes Street where the lights of the city seemed to be glittering solely for our benefit, dismissive of shrill comments that came drifting on the breeze: *Wasn't Harold's reading magnificent! The most wonderful evening ever!* – our only remaining preoccupation now being the 'warmth of a good club with friends'. Secure – finally! – in the knowledge that our fortunes this time had no *option* but to change!

A conviction which, doubtless, brought a smile to the face of the moon as it gazed down from the battlements of the castle, foreordained as it is for that noble sphere to be amused by the affairs of men and their enduringly unstinting belief in themselves. That dogged insistence that things just simply 'cannot get any worse!', an appraisal in this case proving very wrong indeed as we rounded the last corner triumphantly to be greeted by the sodden sign:

CLOSED!!

L'Envoi

It is sad to report that Patrick and his agent aren't colleagues any more. That their journey back to the hotel that night was one fraught with bitter words and recrimination, and that their last lingering belief in the 'philosophy of good things', to coin perhaps a name for it, was savagely obliterated forever when the hotel bar also proved to be closed and their one final hope – the mini-bars – empty.

Nothing would give me greater pleasure than to be able to delineate here how they heroically overcame their difficulties and to this day are often to be observed sharing a glass of Moët & Chandon in the literary haunts of London's metropolis as they laugh almost nostalgically about that 'Edinburgh night'! Which, if things had been otherwise, could have become a little joke.

Except that things weren't otherwise and any time now, if you even mention its name, the author will begin to quiver and a strange look will come in his eye, as though unspooling deep within him is some widescreen mini-Hammer movie, where everything is forever nocturnal and all he can hear is the sinister rolling of thunder and the sudden crack of a lightning bolt as it flashes across the heavens, transcribing for posterity its malevolent, hell-forged rubric:

He went over to Scotland and he thought he'd find fame
But he didn't, the bollocks, because nobody came!

'All is confounded, all!
Reproach and everlasting shame
Sits mocking in our plumes.' Shakespeare, *Henry V*

Adam Thorpe

November, 1988. Laura Cumming of the *Literary Review* on the phone.

'Hi, Adam. Like to do an interview?'

'OK. Who with?'

'Poet. Begins with B.'

'Brownjohn?'

'Brodsky.'

'Jesus.'

'It's the big one. A scoop. Exclusive, too.'

I'd reason to be nervous. Joseph Brodsky had recently won the Nobel Prize for Literature, had spent years in an Arctic labour camp, had been 'adopted' by Auden, wrote long poems in both Russian and English, and was described as 'one of the greatest poets of the twentieth century' (by his publishers). Apart from a pat on the head from the Queen in Calcutta (an event of which I have no memory), I had never in my life encountered anybody as big; it would be like interviewing a cliff.

He was over in London to launch the Penguin edition of

his latest poetry collection, *To Urania*. For the next week I filled my spare hours (I was a full-time lecturer at PCL) with a lot of Brodsky as well as Mandelstam, Akhmatova and Tsvetayeva. I made twenty pages of notes and quotes. Then I boiled down the notes. Like spinach, they boiled down to something that wasn't enough to feed an interviewer for more than about ten minutes. I'd learned that Brodsky had a bristling creative energy, could reel off whole English poems (especially Betjeman's), laughed a lot, and was generally very Russian. This reassured me; all I had to provide was a trigger.

'Always start with a quote,' my English teacher would say. Artfully, I made my first question turn around Auden.

You have called Auden 'a stoic who prays'. Could this also be a self-definition?

He would have to be modest to the point of illness not to rise to that; there would be a gush of passionate memories and reflections. All I had to do was nod and smile.

The morning of the interview, I slipped my own slim volume into the briefcase along with Brodsky's pile, and tested my old portable tape-recorder – I wouldn't be able to keep up with the passionate flood by note-taking, and I wanted an exact transcription. The tape-recorder didn't work. It had worked perfectly for years. I had an hour before the interview at Penguin's headquarters, and I lived out in Bounds Green. Its quiet electrical appliance shop had only one tape-recorder in stock. I made it just on time to the grandiose Penguin headquarters, struggling with my briefcase and the shiny new silver-and-crimson ghetto blaster. The receptionist didn't know anything about an interview. The publicity person was called up. I was told to wait. I sat in a trendy leather chair. A lot of people who looked like Joseph Brodsky passed through the lobby. Everyone had an affable, confident air. After an hour, I

suggested to the receptionist that Mr Brodsky might have forgotten his appointment. I went up in a lift and met the publicity
person and then went down again and waited another hour.
I felt that she hadn't rated the *Literary Review* very highly. The
large ghetto blaster made me look flippant, no doubt.

It was decided, with my encouragement, that Joseph Brodsky wasn't coming. This was confirmed when the man himself
was finally contacted. He was tired or having a good time or
maybe both. He took some persuading, but granted another
interview in two days' time at 'his' place, in Hampstead. I felt
a nuisance.

'Alfred Brendel's house,' sighed the publicity person, putting the phone down. 'They're good friends.'

I pictured Brodsky singing poignant Russian songs at the
home piano of the greatest pianist in the world as I downed
vodkas on the sofa and clapped along. I couldn't imagine being
so famous that one actually turned down exclusive interviews.
It increased Brodsky's status even more. Two days later I was
walking on Hampstead Heath, trying to raise mine. I tested
my voice; it was squeaky with nerves. I passed the house in
Well Walk several times. It was impossibly large, half-hidden
behind venerable foliage.

I rang the bell. The door was opened by two small girls.
They looked at me and burst into giggles. I tried to explain.
Somewhere beyond the hall's gloom a woman's voice was
chattering. The girls, giggling all the while, showed me into a
dark sitting-room with a rumpled sofa, ethnic statues and a
grand piano. I waited for their unseen mother – Lady Brendel,
I assumed – to come off the phone. Now and again, the two
girls ran in to take a look at me, finding me just as funny each
time. After three-quarters of an hour I began to feel helpless.
The phone call went on and on. It was strange being in Alfred

Brendel's house without either of the Brendels knowing. There was a new voice, booming in the hall. The sitting-room door was flung open and Joseph Brodsky strode across the room without stopping or looking at me. He shouted, *'OK! This way!'* He was waving a chicken-leg.

By the time I had picked up my ghetto blaster and briefcase, he had disappeared through another door. I followed. A small landing, stairs going down. No Brodsky. I decided to try the stairs and found myself in a basement bedsit with French windows. Brodsky was walking about, gnawing the chicken-leg as if he hadn't eaten in days. A typewriter with a Cyrillic keyboard showed a poem in progress. He seemed very bad-tempered.

'OK, which magazine are you?'

'The *Literary Review,*' I said.

'Owned by an Arab, no?'

'Em, I think so.'

He grunted disapprovingly, indicating a chair. He threw the chicken-leg away and sat down opposite me. He looked quite like Neil Kinnock, I realized.

'OK. Start.'

I was searching around for a socket, the ghetto blaster's lead being short. He stared at the ghetto blaster.

'What's that?'

'A tape-recorder.'

'What the hell for?'

'To record you.'

'Why?'

He appeared genuinely alarmed. I pictured KGB cells, interrogations with cigarette-ends. I stammered out that I liked to catch precisely what people said, their rhythms and turns of phrase. The man who had been under attack recently for his poems' not-quite-natural English phrasing glared at me. I was bright red.

'Better to use your brain and try to listen,' he growled.

I plugged it in, anyway; it had cost me too much money to waste. I am a worm, I thought. I cleared my throat.

'You have called Auden "a stoic who prays". Could this also be a self-definition?'

'What?'

I repeated the question. My voice sounded even worse, as did the question. He snorted.

'If somebody else would do that, I wouldn't object.'

Silence.

'But you wouldn't describe yourself as that?' I asked, weakly.

'I wouldn't describe myself in any fashion, period.'

Jesus Christ.

'Why is that?'

I was wet with sweat. I wanted to leave.

'I am not interested in myself.'

He chuckled. It was a sardonic chuckle, but it was Russian. It was a tiny light in the darkness. The tiny light grew, if fitfully. He said some memorable things. Larkin was the last of the Roman poets. The novel is the marriage and poetry is the one-night stand, yah? By the end he was almost friendly. I gave him my slim volume and he promised to read it. He nodded towards the French windows. I picked up my briefcase and the ghetto blaster and backed out like an incompetent burglar, but smiling all the way.

'Open thy bowels of compassion.'
Congreve, *The Mourning Bride*

Jonathan Lethem

Book-touring, in America, is a slog. The process is much less
romantic, so much less a coronation, than some might imagine.
It's churlish to complain about the effort of one's publisher to
bring a book to the light of an audience, and I won't complain
here: I'll book-tour again this year, and I'll see many good
friends – booksellers, interviewers, and my publisher's remote
operatives – acquired in earlier rounds. But the net effect is a
slog through a morass of Sartrean repetitions. I begin tours
cheerfully, and end them as a zombie, hoping not to be
ungracious in any number of dazed moments.

I think of my escorts. Not the type found in ads in the back
of weekly newspapers, but 'literary escorts', those local sprites
schlepping writers in and out of airports, hotel lobbies, radio
stations and bookstores. Escorts are not the cause of mortification, but the witnesses to it. They're the human link, the
local flavour. I think of my dear escort in Minnesota, who
drove a battered Toyota, its dashboard decorated with gopher
skulls and dried branches of herb, and who escorted authors

to support finishing an epic, book-length poem on the subject
of roadkill. I remember my Vietnam vet escort in Kansas City,
bravely limping with his cane around the car to open my side
door. I remember many others and love them all.

I think of the radio. The radio is, for me, the void. A tour
consists of waking at five, breakfasting in the airport, landing
in a new city and dropping one's bags in a hotel room, then
being whisked to a radio station to make a nine or ten a.m.
live talk show, where a jaded local host who's read only a
summary of your book and barely learned to pronounce your
name will ask you questions about your mother and father
and whether you know anyone really famous. Later that night
you'll see local friends, you'll read aloud to live humans
who've put aside part of their lives to come and see you stand
at a podium. If you're lucky you'll have a nap in your hotel,
you'll be treated to an elaborate meal – sometimes a good one
– and you'll have time to figure out which city you're in. But
not before you've been put on the radio. When you're talking
on the radio you've had a flight and a coffee in a paper cup
and a crumb of something. You've had time to empty your
bladder – but only your bladder. Then you reply to questions
asked by someone uninterested in the answers, into the whis-
pery microphones of a padded booth. Your listeners, if they
exist, are invisible, distant, and likely missed your name even
if it was pronounced correctly. The radio is the void where
you stare into your own soul on book-tour and find nothing
staring you back.

Once, a particular escort in a particular city came together
with the radio experience, in a way which was not so much
mortifying as edifyingly humbling. She was a big, rowdy,
middle-aged blonde who had been, some years before, the
lead anchorperson on the local news. She'd also obviously

been stunningly beautiful in her youth. She reminded me, immediately and delightfully, of Gena Rowlands in the Cassavetes film *Opening Night* – a character modelled, in turn, on Bette Davis in *All About Eve*. That is to say, a *real star*, made insecure by age. What I couldn't know was that her new job as escort – and I was evidently one of her very first authors – made, by design or accident, a beautiful cure.

We stopped at two or three radio stations that day, and one local television station. It happened at the first stop, and every stop to follow: she was received as a returning comet. From the receptionists to the producers to the technicians to the interviewers themselves, everyone was in awe that she'd swept in – and I was a token at her side, a negligible presence. How good she looked! How they missed her! What a young bimbo they'd replaced her with! How shocking that she'd been cut from the air just for getting a bit older – nobody in this business had any respect any more for the true giants! By dint of my tour itinerary, prepared months before and thousands of miles away in an office in Manhattan, this greatest of local media stars was making her return tour of local media outlets. They fell over themselves for her. Here was true fame, a face they'd gazed at five evenings a week for ten years. I could have been Rushdie, I could have been DeLillo, I could have been T.S. Eliot, it wouldn't have mattered in the least. She took her courtiers graciously, I should add – and was always forgiving when they spoke of the betrayal of her firing. 'Oh, that's just this business, you know how it is . . .'

That's my story, a gentle one. I'm glad to share it. More important, though: I must be certain you understand – you out there, whoever you are, faceless army, listening to morning talk shows. I know you're there somewhere, and I have something to tell you. Those authors you hear at nine or ten in the morning, speaking so tenderly or angrily of their childhood or broken marriage, or meticulously defending their book against this or that possible misunderstanding, or answering unexpected questions about their hair colour or their pets, or explaining why no one will ever know the final truth about what resides in the human heart, you *must know* this: they are holding in a bowel movement.

'When an elephant is in trouble, even a frog will kick him.'
Hindu proverb

Jonathan Coe

One story, of a bad experience in front of the reading public? Just the one? That's impossible. There are far too many to choose from. Just off the top of my head, we have:

– The time when I agreed to appear at a crime writers' festival (Why? I'm not a crime writer), was scheduled to read at the same time as Colin Dexter, and got an audience of precisely one. 'I'm so glad you came along,' I said to the amiable punter, after twenty minutes' chat. 'Think how terrible it would have been if there'd been nobody.' 'Actually,' he admitted, 'I'm the person who was supposed to be introducing you.' (It was Ian Rankin.)

– The time I had another audience of one, in Stamford, Lincs – a sclerotic middle-aged businessman who seemed to have wandered in by mistake – and when I told him I didn't intend to write a novel about the collapse of the Berlin Wall (this was 1989) he started bellowing at me, 'You're a coward, man, a bloody coward!'

– The time I was on a panel discussion on French TV, and the recording over-ran, and knowing that I had to catch the last Eurostar to London I gestured frantically to the floor-manager, and he came over to fetch me but told me to leave unobtrusively, so in order to miss the camera-line I had to crawl off the set on my hands and knees in front of the studio audience, thinking, 'I bet this never happens to Julian Barnes'.

– Signing-queue mortifications: the woman who picked up one of my novels in Brighton, read the author's biog (a functional listing of my previous books), sniffed 'Is that your only claim to fame?' and when I said 'Yes' put the book back on the pile; or the female student (also in Brighton) who sweetly said to me, 'Can I ask you a question?' and when I said 'Yes', demanded briskly, 'Why are all your women characters so crap?'

There are others, even worse, that I have probably suppressed. All helping to form the same resolution, taken time and again: not to put myself through this sort of thing any more. To stay at home, and sit behind my desk, as real writers are supposed to do.

My next scheduled reading is in two days' time.

'This is the posture of fortune's slave: one foot in the gravy, one foot in the grave.' James Thurber

Hugo Hamilton

Nothing could go wrong. I was in charge of the cooking myself. My favourite fish dish – hake with an Asian cross-over flavour, a real winner. I had already tried it out on various guests and each time received this winsome, tearful puppy-look across the table after the first forkful, that simultaneous look of sadness and ecstasy as if to say – you're killing me, this is so delicious. Some people have even uttered dust-jacket terms like amazing, stunning, genius.

Everything was on course for a great night. What could be more exciting than sitting down with another writer, an internationally well-known novelist to whom I had promised dinner in Dublin. She and her husband were in town and coming around for a quiet chat. Just four of us around the table. Lots of shop talk, no complications with mismatched guests, no writer running into vicious reviewer, no awkward questions and nobody saying 'sorry, I haven't read any of your books – yet'. Nothing like the time I was once invited to dinner in Canada myself and sat beside somebody who was fascinated by the fact that I was a writer and then said: 'I know somebody who reads.'

Of course there were the usual pre-dinner anxieties, irrational paranoia that every host experiences over the unlikely odds that you might actually poison your guest with kindness, that they will turn suddenly blue in the face at the whiff of peanuts, do a Saint Vitus dance or just drop dead from the spice. You do your best. After that it's guest beware.

It was none of these things that went wrong on the night. No choking, no spluttering, no famous writer suddenly rushing off to the bathroom. In fact I soon got the familiar nod across the table, the one that makes you feel you've pulled off the great miracle once again by some sheer fluke. Everything was perfect. No big conversation gaffe either, no clanger hanging in the air with an awkward silence.

It was much worse, an own-goal of the most embarrassing kind. The music. I had a CD on low to fill in the background silence. Just a hint of sound leaking out from the speakers to colour the air. Everybody was talking so much, in any case, that you would not even notice who was playing.

Music is the enemy of literature, I recall George Steiner saying at one time. I never realized how true it was until that night. I suppose he meant that the two are so close in nature that they compete like rejected lovers, that music has the edge because it goes straight to the heart. On the night, the music killed everything. The writer I had invited to dinner was beginning to talk about the book she was just about to write, telling us how it involved researching certain human rights issues. Everyone was listening, paying attention to every word. And then, I thought, the music was too loud, an interference, the enemy of writers.

I decided to turn it down. I didn't want to switch it off

altogether, but it needed to be put in its place a little. I picked up the new remote control on the table and zapped, just a tiny touch to allow the writer centre stage. She was in full flow now and we were inhaling every word, nodding, occasionally prompting her to say more.

The music was still too loud. It was Buena Vista Social Club, all the rage and appropriate enough, at the time, to the conversation we were having. But it was overpowering. It sounded like a right fiesta going on in the background, too raucous, too happy and too much of a defiant celebration.

As she continued talking, I picked up the remote control again and discreetly zapped once more. Down. Stay down, music. She looked at me with a strange expression, a little irritated, I thought, as if she didn't want me to turn it down. Everybody loves those dilapidated Cuban bars with the faded paint and slow fan overhead and the musicians pounding out their songs in a great spirit of survival. But hold on, we wanted to hear what this writer was saying.

I zapped again, and this time she seemed even more surprised than before. She stopped talking for a moment. Her husband looked up in shock. What I failed to realize was that I was actually turning the music up, instead of down. With great subtlety, I was increasing the volume each time, pressing the wrong button so that the music was getting louder and louder. As if I had no interest in her new book. As if I was hinting that any half-forgotten old musician from Cuba had more in his little finger than three hundred pages of her next novel.

It wasn't true of course. I was immensely interested and kept nodding, despite the jubilant rhythm which was now blasting out like a persistant menace, telling us to dance instead of talk. This time I decided I would turn the volume right down. I mean, there is a time for music and a time for talking. I took the zapper one last time and squeezed my thumb on the button with great vigour. Down, you guys in Havana. We're trying to talk here. Instead, they suddenly came to a proper jazz band, blasting and hooping. Brass instruments yelping like profane circus. It was deafening.

Only then did I realize what I was doing. I immediately corrected and switched off the music altogether. I tried a lame apology, but there was a look of hurt shock in her eyes. She stopped talking. She said she didn't really like talking about her work.

'Calamities are of two kinds: misfortune to ourselves, and good fortune to others.' Ambrose Bierce

Claire Messud

It took me four and a half years to write my second novel, a seemingly endless span endured in relative isolation in Washington DC, where I had few friends (none of them literary), precious little money, and barely any outside employment. Every so often, I would stop work on the novel and, in a fit of despair, apply for jobs – a fair number of them over the years: teaching jobs, management consulting jobs and everything in between – but I was so clearly unsuitable for the wider world that I never got so much as a rejection letter in return.

In the spring of 1998, however, when I finally finished my manuscript, I felt that my fortunes were at last shifting. My agent seemed pleased with the book, and suggested that others might be also. And I had a publication in the offing: Francis Ford Coppola's magazine *Zoetrope* had commissioned a short story, which was soon to appear. More than that, they had invited me to read from it at a trendy Greenwich Village bar, in honour of the magazine's new issue. I was told that I would be reading with another, earlier contributor, whom I shall call

Z, a young woman whose *Zoetrope* short story had earned her
a six-figure book contract and minor celebrity; but I somehow,
wilfully and woefully misguidedly, understood that the reading was primarily in honour of my *Zoetrope* issue, and hence,
by extension, of me.

As I packed my overnight bag for the metropolis, I indulged
in minor, oh-so-careful, fantasies. I didn't imagine a book contract that would make the news, like Z's, but I did imagine
the trendy bar filled with eager readers, *my* eager readers,
perhaps among them editors enamoured of my novel manuscript and prompted, by the wild (although discreet) success
of my short story and reading, to up their offers by a considerable sum. I didn't allow myself to imagine film deals (I wasn't
unreasonable!); but I did see, somehow, in this visit to New
York, a new stage in my life beginning, the end of my literary
isolation and my warm, if belated, welcome into the embrace
of the New York literary scene. This – I could feel it – was the
beginning of my real literary life.

As it happened, the day slated for the auction of my novel
was the same as the day of my reading at the trendy Village
bar. It was a Wednesday, and a memorable one; although not
memorable quite as I might have hoped. The day was not filled
with the frenzied ringing of cell phones around the city, nor with
the pounding of virtual gavels as the auction reached its height.
Rather, it was a day of ever more widely spaced and ever more
sober calls from my agent, informing me that one after another
and then, as the afternoon proceeded, in clutches and clumps,
the editors who were to have raved over my novel were, one by
one, quietly declining to bid. By the end of the afternoon, as I
readied myself to go downtown, to step into the literary spotlight, I had amassed ten rejections, and had none left to go.
Ten submissions, ten rejections. Busy day.

My agent, however, being a marvellous and God-like man, knew exactly what to say: 'Don't worry about it,' he assured me. 'We'll find the right home for your book.' (Which he did, not long after.) 'You know, Beckett was very hard to sell, too.' Which false flattery proved exactly what my bruised ego required to enable me to put on my make-up and high heels and head for my reading. I felt my humiliation was at least private, and my chance for glory, while diminished, not entirely extinguished.

Until, that is, I got to the bar. There, the joint was, as I had spent the long train journey imagining, jumping. Filled to the rafters. Bursting at the seams. Except that the posters, everywhere apparent, from the street outside to the podium at which the reading was to take place, all bore only one typed name: Z's. In big, bright letters: Z's name. My name was there, it's true, hastily scrawled underneath by hand, in some instances misspelled, in others frankly illegible. I was the afterthought, the charity case, the one who shouldn't have been there. And all the fans I'd dreamed about – they were her fans, of course. Just as the book contract and the celebrity and the film deal I hadn't even dared to imagine were hers, too. And to top it off, Z seemed a perfectly pleasant person.

As I pushed my way through the crowd to make myself known to the bar staff, I ran into another young novelist I'd met once before, a member of the hip metropolitan set. 'Are you a friend of Z's too?' he asked. 'Is that why you're reading with her? How's everything going, anyway?'

To which, fool that I was, in my shell-shocked desperation, I told the truth. 'Actually, I've had kind of a rough day,' I said. 'My novel's been turned down ten times since this morning.'

From the expression on his face, you would have thought I'd announced that I had leprosy, or Ebola, or SARS. While striving to retain his society grin, he winced and flinched and grimaced; and I realized the depth of my mistake. Failure is not simply inadmissible, it can be catching. People not only don't want to be failures, they don't want to know them.

But this ambitious young writer knew what to do, in order to inoculate himself and those around him from the threat that I posed. While still flinching and wincing and smiling all at once he said – his only acknowledgement of my confession – 'Wow.' And then, 'Have you met A?' – he grabbed the shoulder of the woman, or girl, beside him and spun her around to face me. She had a great mass of dark curls, and was barely of legal drinking age. 'She's just sold a book of stories this week for $150,000 and she hasn't even finished it yet. Isn't that incredible?'

'Incredible. Congratulations.'

I even smiled. I was polite. I stood up, when my turn came, and read from my story. I slipped out afterwards without speaking to anyone, and took a cab uptown. I made it through.

Years and publications later, I was invited back to the trendy bar, this time to read with a writer in her fifties, as hip a New York writer as someone in her fifties can be. I knew her slightly, and felt fine about the event: it would, I thought, put old ghosts to rest, show me how far I had come.

My husband came with me this time, and this writer blithely called him by someone else's name, repeatedly, in conversation before the reading; by which I should have felt the inauspicious vibe. This writer had asked if she could read first; and of course I agreed. But I was somewhat surprised when, at the intermission, she came to me, her own husband in tow, both with anxious expressions.

'How long do you think you might read for?' she asked.

We'd both been asked to read fifteen minutes. 'Same as you,' I said. 'About fifteen minutes.'

She winced and flinched, though not as dramatically as the young fellow of years before. 'Oh God, this is really embarrassing, but you won't mind if we have to go, will you? It's just that we've got to get home–'

Her husband interrupted her, his hands out like plates in a gesture of plaintive helplessness. '*Sopranos* night,' he said, with a shrug.

The writer had the good grace, at least, to blush like a beetroot, in spite of her hip leather jacket, her downtown persona, her whole cool schtick. But she didn't stay for my reading.

Next time I'm invited to read at the trendy bar in Greenwich Village, I hope I'll know better than to go.

'It is no use trying to tug the glacier backwards.' Tibetan proverb

Michael Bracewell

It all began one wet night in Rochdale, during the late autumn of 1993, at a dingy recording studio called Suite Sixteen. I had come to visit Mark E. Smith – the ex-Communist, former docker, and founder of one of the most innovative groups to emerge in contemporary music, The Fall. With an engineer he was mixing a new album, *Middle Class Revolt*, and he looked as though he'd been up for days. He was, in fact, unconscious when I first arrived – stretched out on the kind of broken-down sofa that you might see outside a mini-cab office on a warm summer evening. Waking, he had seemed immediately to pull all the strands of himself together, acquiring a coherence – like the shards of a Cubist portrait suddenly shooting back into their figurative state – which somehow denied that he'd ever been asleep.

A class warrior, dandy and intellectual, Smith is one of nature's aristocrats. Born and raised in Salford, he is now resident in Prestwich, north Manchester. His performances with The Fall – delivering the elaborate code of his lyrics in plosive, spoken bursts from the corner of his mouth, across rigid, relentless repetitions of rock chords – can seem virtually shamanic. He is Beuysian in this respect. He is also famously acerbic.

Example: a music paper once decided that it would make an interesting story to have various rock celebrities take a train journey together, their wit and conversation being noted down by a journalist. Smith arrived carrying two plastic bags filled with cans of lager, and settled in for the duration. Some hours later, one of the assembled stars was attempting to prove that he had the ability to read a stranger's personality, simply by studying their face. Smith sat in silence throughout the demonstration. Had the amateur analyst been more accomplished, he might have noticed that Smith's eyes had narrowed a fraction – always a bad sign. But at first, all seemed well. 'I can do that, mate,' Smith announced, amiably enough. 'Okay, Mark,' came the bright reply, 'tell me all about myself!'

'You're a cunt.'

Stories such as these had passed into legend. So much so, I felt, that they began to caricature Mark E. Smith as a kind of Alf Garnett of punk rock – obscuring his brilliance as an artist and icon who, on the one hand, had been implored by Kurt Cobain to support his group Nirvana, and on the other invited to address Oxford University's James Joyce society. Smith's work made a mockery of the distinctions between 'high' and 'low' art, or between populism and post-modernism. Thus, entangled in questions of cultural status, I took him out for dinner at an Italian restaurant in Rochdale – where he ate a rabbit – and invited him to be the subject of a public interview, to be conducted by myself, at the Institute of Contemporary Arts in London.

In retrospect, I must have seemed like one of those eager

young reporters from the early days of the BBC – tweedy and hopelessly bourgeois, yet ravenous to engage with the true avant-garde. My admiration for Mark's work knew – and knows – no bounds. Over dinner his anecdotes were hilarious, his insights fascinating: how Nico – the former chanteuse with the Velvet Underground – had once tried to buy some speed off his mum, for instance; and how he was opposed to Manchester's proposed celebration of L.S. Lowry – 'He was a fuckin' rent collector, him: "Come out or I'll paint yer!"' '

Tickets for the event sold well; so well, in fact, that it was moved from the upstairs gallery to the 250-seat theatre. On the night, the audience filled the lobby bar and café, their chatter rising in an anticipatory buzz. A smell of damp cardboard, roll-ups and spilt beer announced the presence of the music press. The talk was scheduled to start at 8 p.m. At 7.45 the Talks Co-ordinator remained calm and cheerful, despite the absence of Mark E. Smith. A veteran of many ICA events, where feuding semioticians had come to blows, for instance, or distinguished speakers on Middle Eastern affairs had arrived unable to speak a word of English, there was little, I thought, that could flap her self-possession. But by 7.55 she was looking slightly clammy.

The metallic clatter of a stage door announced Mark's arrival. He was wearing a grey raincoat and looked sort of blurred around the edges. Unsmiling at our fools' masks of sheer relief, his first request – aimed directly at the undisputedly well-bred Talks Co-ordinator – was for a bucket. To her undying credit, she treated this as the harmless whim of an eccentric genius. A bucket was found. After she had handed it to him, he put it on the floor in front of us and pissed into it, noisily.

By now, the murmur of the audience – there were maybe

two women there, the rest were men – was becoming restless. Backstage, too, was getting tense. At ease in the shabby little dressing room, however, Mark lit a cigarette. His temper was hard to gauge: we were both in this together, it seemed, with parity, as comrades – but at the same time I felt that I was little more than a fledgling in his palm. I would have done well to remember the first quotation of his I had ever written down; 'I like to keep The Fall at arm's length . . .' it began. Then there was Mark's widely publicized relationship with intoxicants and stimulants. Was he on anything? Worse, was he coming down off something? If I'd been Nick Kent, I'd have known. As it was I fiddled with my watch while Mark drank lagers and offered to massage my shoulders. The best part of an hour passed, with increasingly urgent visits from the Talks Co-ordinator. Were we ready yet? 'Right then,' Mark announced, at a little after 9 p.m., and for the first and last time I followed Mark E. Smith out on to a stage.

Some generous applause, and no small amount of heckling greeted our arrival. We had kept the audience waiting – beer-less, unable to smoke – for the best part of an hour and a quarter. Then all was silence.

There is something about the sheer speed with which a public event can suddenly go wrong. There are a few seconds of cold, broiling panic in the pit of your stomach, as you realize that you have just walked – or bounced, even, with the suave smile of the self-assured – into a room that has no floor. I had experienced other dead drops into public humiliation – that occasion on live trans-Danubian radio, for instance, when the presenter had announced, in perky, Americanized English, 'And tonight in the studio we're honoured to welcome Brett Easton Ellis' – but never before in front of an audience.

The hush had been anticipatory, as though a mob were

waiting for the axe to fall. Yet still, incredibly, I maintained a belief that the interview could succeed. It was only when I began to speak – an introductory address I had prepared about Jim Morrison's public interview at the ICA, back in the late sixties – that I suddenly realized how terminally fogeyish, how toxically Middle English, I seemed in that situation. The effect was as though A.N. Wilson had taken to the stage at the 100 Club. The audience began to snigger, first in isolated guffaws and then with abandon. I would see from the photograph in the following day's *Independent* newspaper, that their hilarity was first prompted by the manner in which Mark was sitting beside me, swigging from a bottle of lager, but with his little finger crooked – a savage caricature of gentility: the class warrior unleashed on the twerpish agent of gentrification.

I remembered too late that these kinds of events – 'In Conversations', bookshop appearances and so forth – are wholly bourgeois in their conception: they presuppose a complicity between the audience, subject and interviewer, in which a kind of broadsheet notion of edification is the predominant tone. And I was face to face with the man who had written 'Prole Art Threat' in 1979 and thrown Courtney Love off a tour bus. A man who preferred to get arrested by the LAPD rather than put out his fag on a plane. Smith had lambasted all the institutions of middle-class popular culture, from open-air festivals to student vegans; and as his greatest hero was Wyndham Lewis, so he assumed his best-known public mask of being The Enemy. No matter that I'd seen The Fall maybe twenty times, and no matter that I listened to the records with unceasing enthusiasm, and written about them as vital works of contemporary art. I came across like Wilfrid Hyde-White trying to interview Eminem.

It occurred to me that I had missed the point of The Fall

by a mile. Of course, I should have realized that shamanic class warriors don't do cosy, ICA-style interviews; they operate on a different level, ceaselessly self-protective and necessarily resistant to the commodifying grasp – the pasteurizing process – of institutional cultural interpretation. I'd watched Jean Genet on the *South Bank Show*, refusing to comply with the probings of polite mediation. For Smith to become the amiable studio guest, offering insights into his creative method, would have undermined the purpose of his entire project. But that realization came later. 'Can you remember the early concerts in the working men's clubs?' I asked, fingering my notes with sweating hands; ' 'Course I can. Do you think I'm daft?' came the sharp reply. 'Were you always interested in music?' 'My uncle played the saw. Lovely instrument.' And so on. The remaining fifty minutes became a dark vortex – somewhere in the diminishing perspectives of which I took temporary leave of my body.

Some years later, I asked the ICA for a copy of their tape of the event. Listening to it, I was overwhelmed by just how generous, eloquent, affectionate and informative Mark had actually been during the interview. But there had been some fundamental collision of expectations and attitudes, between audience, speaker and event, which had all but drowned out the talk itself: to have thought of the public interview with Mark in terms of blurring cultural boundaries, had proved pointless. As Ken Dodd once remarked, 'Try telling Freud's theory of humour to the second house at the Glasgow Empire on a Saturday night.'

In addition to which, the turbulence which the event had seemed to summon up – a volatility of ambience which Elvis Presley's biographer, Albert Goldman, once described as 'acoustic steam' – was perhaps a version of the same intensity which Smith brings to his performances with The Fall – as though his personality becomes a poltergeist, once he hits the stage. At the end of the talk, questions from the audience had turned nasty. 'Mark, are you still a drunk?' some man asked from the side of the darkened auditorium.

This comes pretty near the end of the tape. 'Gotta split,' Mark replies; and the void left by his departure from the stage, as recorded, is a rising roar of static electricity.

'Insults should be well avenged or well endured.' Spanish proverb

Darryl Pinckney

More than ten years ago I went on a national reading tour to promote the paperback edition of the novel I'd published the year before. The tour had its strange, moody hosts, its moments of validation from audiences, the schedule of fast-moving evenings that give you a Friendliness Hangover when it's all over and done with, because you've talked so much and wanted to be liked so much you've tried to become best friends with everyone you met. The tour also had its forlorn venues. In Atlanta, during a terrible storm, the manager of the suburban bookstore where I was to appear assured me that it was not my fault that I was not Madonna and could not attract a crowd in such weather. Thunder rattled the panes. The shop was near empty. By 8.15 there were three black people seated in the front row; the rest of the chairs were vacant. Two white customers, sussing that a boring, poorly attended reading was about to take place, dived down the aisle toward the shelf of tax manuals. One of the three black people said that they ran an experimental theatre in Atlanta and knew the experience of finding more people on stage than in the audience, so if I wanted to read then they were prepared to listen. I hoped that anecdote would entertain and move the people in the publicity department back at my publishers. I had an obscure fear of them.

A few days later, in misty Portland, Oregon, I met up with an English friend, a poet, who the day before had read to an audience of 3000 in a downtown Portland theatre. Surprising, wonderful, cultured, hippy Portland. As my friend and I entered the bookshop where I was to give a reading, I put the paperback copy of my book in my pocket. Then this weird thing happened: 'Hey!' I paid no attention. 'Excuse me, I'm talking to you.' I turned about and saw a clerk, his tag around his neck. 'Could you step this way, please?' That was a rather brusque way to invite me to sign books, I thought. But, no, the clerk wanted to know if I'd just slipped something into my pocket. Yes. But that was all I was going to say. The clerk wanted to see what I had just slipped into my pocket. I saw the sign above the cashiers' station, a sign that warned shop-lifters that they would be prosecuted. My friend barked, 'He's reading here tonight!' He couldn't believe it either. I was being stopped as a suspected shoplifter. I know a painter who refuses to have anything to do with a canvas once he's decided it's finished. He wants his gallery to take it away and sell it as quickly as possible. The painting must begin its own life, one independent of the artist, immediately. The clerk didn't blink at the photograph of the black guy on the back cover of the copy of *High Cotton* in my unsteady hand. My friend was going ballistic. I fled. I went outside for a cigarette. Someone came and got me when it was time for me to go on. I didn't see that clerk. My friend sat in the rear, fuming. Otherwise, my audience amounted to about thirty people, seven of them either high-school classmates or the siblings of classmates. But I had a great time after all and I wanted the publicity department back at my publishers to be glad to hear it. As he held the door for us, the bookstore manager made apologies to my friend again. He'd really scared them, which nicely covered up for what I like to pretend was my complicated lack of reaction to being asked to frisk myself in a bookstore.

'He that riseth late must trot all day.' Benjamin Franklin

Irvine Welsh

I'm very fortunate in that I'm not that easily embarrassed, which is a good thing as my behaviour has often not been up to scratch, this particularly being the case in my youth. I think that, over the years, I've become inured to the type of embarrassment that really fucks some other people up. I'm not sure whether this is a good or bad thing. Like most of us, the bulk of my cringe-worthy moments have come about through intoxication on drink or drugs. Now I've got to the point that I get somewhat red-faced if I wake up to find out that I *haven't* made a complete tit of myself. It always seems a waste of a night out.

Of course, although it certainly helps, I don't need drink and drugs to make an absolute prick of myself. Even sober, I'm the master of the *faux pas*. I blame this on the incredible arrogance of being so wrapped up in myself that I can't be bothered to pay attention to what's going on around me. Once, when I had taken a new job in London, after the first week my boss took me out for a drink. It was a relaxed, cordial affair although the alcohol was slipping down a bit quickly. He asked me if I was enjoying the job. I told him that it was fine. He then asked if I was getting on with everybody at work. I explained that they were all very nice, but there was one woman manager who worked upstairs. I told him that everybody hated her, thought she was a 'poisonous cunt'. At this point I perhaps should have noticed the slightly pained, if thoughtful, reaction on my boss's face.

The next day, suitably vulnerable and hung-over, I was having a lunchtime game of pool with a girl who worked upstairs beside the woman in question. She asked me if I'd had a good time last night. I told her that I did, but I'd had more to drink than I thought I would. She asked me about the boss and how I got on with him. I told her that I thought that he seemed a really nice guy. (It was very unusual for me to feel that way about any boss I've had.) She agreed that he was okay, but then she said, 'It must be strange for him to be working so closely with his wife . . .' Of course, I knew straight away whom she meant by this, experiencing what myself and a good friend called 'the crumbling dam effect'. This occurs when you feel your face suddenly collapse in response to, well, mortification.

This type of embarrassment is intense, but relatively routine. The big problem in trying to dredge up a really mortifying memory is that there are so many and you suspect that you've repressed the best (or worst) ones. Anyway, one that always sticks in my mind was when I was ticketless at the Scotland v. England game at Wembley in 1979. I sat with two friends and a huge carry-out in the car park outside the stadium. We had been in a state of alcoholic oblivion for a few days and we wouldn't have thanked anybody for tickets at that point, we just wanted to finish our session.

I farted and followed through. Despite the quickening of the pulse and sweating of the brow in response to the warm feeling in my underpants, I nonchalantly headed up and off to the toilets in Wembley Way. I thought that I would defecate, get cleaned up best I could, probably flushing my keks away if the damage proved to be too bad.

The problem was I found that the toilets had been so badly vandalized that they looked like the footpath at Edinburgh's Royal Commonwealth Pool. Only they had a couple of inches of pishy water all over the floor, which you had to paddle through to get to the toilet traps, urinals and sinks. My hole-ridden trainers wouldn't stand a chance, so I took them off, then my socks. Rolling up my jeans, I paddled along to a smashed up toilet-bowl. I then shat and wiped myself with the clean portion of my underpants. (There was no toilet paper.) I jettisoned the pants and took off my jeans and paddled my way to a wash-hand basin. As, naked from the waist down, I tried to wash out my arse, a group of Weedgies stood at the entrance, just pishing into the toilet and laughing loudly at my predicament. I carried on with as much dignity as one can muster in such circumstances, climbing up onto these boxed-in pipes and washing my piss-soaked feet in the sink. Then I scrambled along the ledge to the door and jumped out emerging into the car-park, where to the laughter of loads of drunken football supporters, I pulled on my jeans, socks and trainers.

I left the scene as quickly as I could and walked round the stadium to compose myself. On my return to our drinking camp, an irate pal asked me where I had been. I explained that there was a big queue in the toilets. At this point I really thought that I'd got out of jail. I had been embarrassed – brutally, shamefully embarrassed – but I'd never see those people again in my life. We'd get back to my flat where I'd change into fresh keks before going out again and this time I'd switch from lager to Guinness. Just as I was feeling a little bit pleased with myself, I heard a shout go up, quite close: 'Hey, there's Shitey-Pants!' It was the Weedgies who'd witnessed my plight in the toilets, now laughing again and pointing me out to their pals. They gathered round and with great delight started filling my friends in with the details. For years, the story of my Wembley humiliation was a favourite amusement in several London and Edinburgh bars. Aye, that one still haunts me. One day I'll write about it . . .

'A Poet is the most unpoetical of anything in existence; because he has no Identity – he is continually informing – and filling some other Body.'
Keats, letter to Richard Woodhouse, Oct. 27, 1818

Andrew Motion

It was early 1977, a few months after I'd started lecturing in English at Hull, and I was trying to revive the university's Poetry Society, which had sunk into one of its occasional lethargies. I'd asked some big names to come and give readings, and most of them had said yes – mistakenly thinking the time and trouble of getting to the campus would be rewarded by an encounter with Larkin. And (as you do) I'd also invited some less well-known people. Carol Rumens, then near the start of her writing life, was one of these; I'd never met her, but I liked her work and thought she'd add some range and surprise to the series. I arranged to collect her off the train from London, thinking there'd be no difficulty about this. The journey was long but straightforward, and I'd be able to recognize her, having seen her author photo.

So there I was at 6.30 at Hull Paragon scanning the faces as her train pulled in. And there was Carol, slightly taller than I expected, wearing a pair of glasses she'd obviously bought since the photo-shoot, carrying an overnight case and a shoulder-bag which presumably held her poems. I greeted her, explained we had time to get something to eat before the reading began, and led her towards the taxi rank. She looked slightly bemused but only slightly, and didn't say much. That was okay. I'd heard she was shy, and anyway I was the one who had to do the talking; she needed to compose herself. 'Where will I be staying?' was her only question, and I explained there was a hotel just across the road from the university.

It seemed like a good idea to avoid much mention of the reading – that might make her nervous, and would in turn feed her shyness. So we chatted about ordinary things – the journey, the bizarrely beautiful name of Hull's station, the city – and eventually took our seats in an Indian restaurant. Here our small talk started to run out and poetry became more or less unavoidable. Whom did she know? What kind of stuff did she like? Evidently not much. In fact, judging by her mumbles as she fiddled with the menu and then her specs and then the menu again, the whole subject of poetry was not one she enjoyed. Oh well. 'I too dislike it,' I told her, meaning to be affable, and explained that the previous week we'd had Geoffrey Hill over from Leeds. He didn't seem to like much either.

'Geoffrey Hill?'

'Yes, you know, Carol. Geoffrey Hill. *King Log. Mercian Hymns.*'

Her menu was on the table now, and she leaned back in her chair. 'What makes you think I'm called Carol?'

'It's your name, isn't it?'

'My name's Natalie.'

'But I thought . . .'

'I know what you thought.'

'But I didn't . . . And anyway, you didn't have to . . .'

I fled. Apologised and fled. Back to the station, and the sight of the real Carol leaning against a pillar, waiting for me – the Carol who was just the height I expected, and still had the same pair of specs she'd worn for her photograph. I didn't have the heart to explain why I was so late collecting her – at least not then, as she was about to give a reading, the very time when she would want to feel confident, most securely *herself*. But I did tell her later, and said I'd felt, well, mortified. She forgave me. As for Natalie, who knows?

'When there is yet shame, there may in time be virtue.'
Samuel Johnson

Karl Miller

Philosophers have thought about the difference between shame and guilt and about the difference between a shame culture and a guilt culture. For my part, I haven't been able to get beyond the untutored view that shame is likely to be a result of the public exposure of an act experienced by the actor as wrong, but that the two states are often indistinguishable. Mortifications have been defined as shames or ignominies, but they needn't be public. They can be felt in unrelieved secrecy, in the silence of your room.

One of mine came early and lasted for the rest of my life. I was in the Army at the time, doing my basic training as a National Serviceman and a sapper, a Royal Engineer. I was to be seen lying on my bed, or standing by it to attention, in a creosoted hut or 'spider' near Farnborough in Hampshire, or sallying out to march up and down and stamp my feet. My platoon was ruled by two men rather more unlike one another than shame and guilt tend to be. The lance-corporal was gentle, lean and elegant, nothing like the raving bullies among the parade-ground NCOs. He was an East Anglian waterman in civilian life, and would tell us what it was to be rowing or poling the Fens. The corporal was the bad cop, not given to reminiscence, miles less endearing than the man from the marshes, but with a hint of these in his looks: an old young man with thinning hair, a round, muddy, doughy face, piercing brown eyes and a croaking wire-cutter voice.

There arose this issue of weekend passes, which took you for thirty-six hours out of your spider, bound for the brief encounter. You had to queue and sue and plead for a pass. This particular weekend, one savourless Saturday morning in a camp deserted save for a few left-behind conscripts and their minders, I was still hoping, with time running out, for a trip to London to see a woman old enough to be my mother. I set myself to argue my case, which clashed with the claims of another sapper, a shy man. The corporal let go with a fiercely moral diatribe about cutting in and jumping the queue, every word of which I believed. I felt guilty and ashamed.

The corporal hated me and my brief encounter, hated me for trying to parlay a respite at someone else's expense. And I hated me for it too, though I'm not sure that shoving someone aside had been a feature of my conscious intention. I apologize for an unhappy lack of the lurid in this confession, and hope to do a bit better presently. I have certainly performed many worse actions. Why then have I held on for so long to this memory of the Farnborough disgrace?

I think it was a device for not thinking about what was worse, an ongoing worse. None of my early mortifications shows me in a very bad light: they are more like embarrassments than disgraces, revealing inexperience and, in this case, a less than Hitlerian will to power, and their reverberations are like a cover story for actions that came later. But this durable memory may also testify to an idea of fairness which is always around but was especially cogent during the war and after it. I was not shamed for this action before the other soldiers, and the shy sapper didn't seem to mind. They recognized that you had to stick your neck out and push your luck, at times, under the Army's regime of insult and frazzling punctilio. But there was also then, more than now, a sense that you shouldn't take advantage, or steal a march, and it was this sense that stung me, and stung me. Advantage became more of an option for people in the years to come. Ahead lay a familiarity with the chief executive who receives a salary of millions and a proportionate bonus when he brings down his firm.

No one would expect an unclouded fairness from custodians of good order and military discipline, and this was as true then, in the Forties, as it is now. But I remember Farnborough as a better place than the camp at Deepcut, with its recent bullyings, mysterious deaths and attempted cover-up. There were only two deaths not caused by enemy action during my days as a soldier, one of them the reported stamping on a homosexual man by Scottish Territorials on the spree at a summer camp.

In the Scotland where I grew up there was plenty of room for the survival of a guilt culture whereby pleasure was hard to excuse and homosexuality an outlandish evil. Hostility, contempt, violence of the tongue or boot, were accounted less deadly than the sexual sins, in parts and patches of the country, and there were those people by whom poverty was considered a disgrace. An earlier mortification, suffered at the age of fifteen, made me aware of the importance of sexual misconduct. A teacher summoned me to his classroom to ask what I knew of homosexual behaviour rumoured of one of the school's sportsmen. I don't believe I knew anything; this was the time when I'd had to look the word up in a dictionary, after a reading of Aldous Huxley. But I felt guilty about being consulted, and about feeling grave and consequential during the interview. A year or so before this, a teacher, with a sad and swampy dough face quite like the corporal's, had chosen to sew a fly-button on my shorts. I seem to recall that this was experienced as a shame, on social grounds, because of that missing button, by the kindly 'guardians' with whom I lived – my parents had been separated at birth, *my* birth. My guardians felt, I think, that we had been shown up. I was not amused, and not aroused, by the sewing session. I was bemused. I couldn't even look it up in the dictionary.

Guilt has receded in a world where there is more to be guilty of. War is even worse, more unprincipled in its execution, than it was when I narrowly missed waging it. Guilt has become unpopular, can be thought ugly, unhealthy, with the splendours of the Victorian conscience long since seen as shams, and so on. It seems to me that it's worth enduring if it helps you, though it often doesn't, to be unto others 'as you'd have others be to you', in the words of my grandmother Georgina's sampler. The poet Auden had words to say (before he softened them) about a 'conscious acceptance of guilt in the necessary murder'. This description of Auden's eventually renounced histrionic political Thirties might lead one to consider the bullying unelected American President of the present day, who can look like his worst enemies – full of blame and bad at feeling guilty. But he can also look as if he is capable of it. And guiltiness can reasonably be suspected of a degree of complicity in the 'necessary murders' of the past.

There was a nineteenth-century admiration of Thomas Carlyle which rushed to agree with him that 'we are all wrong and all like to be damned'. Feeling, and blaming others for being, guilty as hell has given guilt a bad name. But let's just go on feeling it. It can appear to be a way of trying to find the plot, to know what you are doing, and have been driven to do. Not the only way, though. The waterman I met in the Army seemed to know what he was doing, where to steer his boat and how to weather the Army. But I don't suppose he was ever to make much use of the rudder of self-incrimination. I hope you are still with me.

While writing this piece, I dreamt that my mother had died in some sort of car mishap on the doorstep of the house of one of my sons. Round I went to kiss the blood that stained the pavement. There's a possible Scots mortification or compunction here, to do with telling such a dream, confessing the kiss. But I don't feel that, or approve of that. For me, the mortification is not being able in old age, when your middle years are apt to vanish, to remember my mother's death.

I notice that my piece on mortification has turned into a family matter. The ability to be pained by what you've done has many faces, a touchingly capacious repertoire, ranging from compunction to contrition and the drama of remorse. They seem to include the guilt of the elderly child of parted parents.

'Art is a human product, a human secretion, it is our body that sweats the beauty of our works.' Émile Zola

Michael Longley

In his more curmudgeonly mode John Hewitt once said to me: 'If you write poetry, it's your own fault.' By extension, if you are vainglorious enough to consider your poems and your plangent drone sufficiently titillating to tempt the punters from their firesides, then you should be beyond mortification. But of course none of us is.

Reciting my kind of lyric poetry requires being private in public without embarrassing either the listeners or myself. Once in a while I feel so discomfited I perspire Satchmo-style, sweat stinging my eyes and percolating through my whiskers onto the page. Apart from passing out or running away, there is no escape. I stand there stammering while self-humiliation irrigates the sheugh of my arse.

More often it is your supposed admirers who stoke up the self-doubt. Here are a few examples:

driving the length of Ireland to Wexford to read to no one. 'You coincide with the opera,' the two young organizers explained;

in North Carolina locking myself in my host's lavatory
– breaking the lock – and having to climb through the
window and down a ladder to get to my reading;

in a Tokyo university reading to an audience of one, the
Dean of the Faculty of Humanities;

being introduced by Fred Johnston in Galway as 'quite well-
known' (true, but a somewhat detumescent overture);

in Arizona being announced thus: 'With an audience like
this one, Michael Langley requires no introduction';

at the Cuirt Festival in Galway being interrupted mid-
flow by an American voice: 'Why are you so bitter?' (Hm,
yes, why?);

at the end of a reading in New York being asked by
an ancient bag-lady: 'Why don't you read like Dylan
Thomas?' (Hm, yes, why not?);

prior to a group reading in Derry being cornered by a
pretty young woman with tears in her eyes: 'Are you
Michael Longley?' A fan, I thought. 'May I shake your
hand?' A fan indeed. Glad hand proffered. 'I've always
wanted to shake the hand of the man to whom Seamus
Heaney dedicated "Personal Helicon".'

Mortification can cut two ways. Poetry readings used to be
launched on a tidal wave of alcohol. Long ago in the seventies
I was giving a joint reading at the Morden Tower in Newcastle.
I was pie-eyed but, unfortunately, not yet paralytic. I could

still stand up and communicate in a rudimentary fashion. I introduced my first poem and then went on introducing it. After more than twenty disconnected minutes I crumpled into my seat without reading a single line. I don't know who my co-reader was. I can't remember anything. A friend who was present tells me that someone made a tape-recording of my preposterous wittering. May it unravel and autodestruct as I did.

About the same time, I shared a poetry reading with James Simmons at Trinity College, Dublin, my alma mater. I had been an undistinguished student, but did not choose this occasion to make amends. The setting was more professional than it often is: two chairs, a lectern, a table, glasses of water, sympathetic lighting. I think I read first. I was in my cups. While Jimmy was up at the lectern reading his poems and singing his songs, I dropped off and started to snore. A sodden drone. A floodlit kip. Jimmy told me afterwards that I had snored all the way through his performance. 'Why didn't you wake me up?' 'You were making such a lovely rhythmic sound.'

Next comes post-reading mortification – more drink at the home of the resigned, forbearing host. On the campus of a great American university at a reception in my honour I challenged a world expert on the life and poetry of Robert Frost. A Guinness and whiskey man, I had forgotten that dry martinis consist of more than fortified wine. In no time at all I was telling the professor that he knew fuck-all about Frost or anything else. My host tried to humour me by suggesting that I recite one of my own poems. I wobbled through 'The Linen Industry' to the penultimate line but, with the end in sight, found myself back at the beginning. This happened three or four times. Refusing to step off my demented roundabout, I was led by the elbow upstairs to bed.

There were worse readings and worse receptions. They have vanished into the black hole of alcoholic amnesia. I was not an alcoholic, just a practitioner of what in Belfast we call 'serious drinking'. After the deluge of a St Patrick's Day bender in 2000 I decided to jump off the deadly dull merry-go-round. I haven't had a drink for more than three years. Mortification still comes my way, but less frequently.

Hugo Williams

I received a package in the post containing my American travel book, *No Particular Place to Go*, a stamped addressed envelope and a letter from someone in Warwick requesting my signature, or, if possible, a signed photo of myself. She enclosed a few of her poems, in case I was interested. She didn't want to put me to any trouble. I signed the book and had a look at the poems. They were good in a very up-to-date, knowing sort of way, mostly about sex. I wrote a few suggestions on them, then sent everything back with a complimentary letter and a photo of myself. The following week she wrote back saying she was putting a collection together and wondered if I would mind casting an eye over it before she sent it off. I agreed to this, adding that I would like a signed photograph of her. I knew that she would recognize this request from a story in my travel book in which I ask for an American fan's photo, only to be met off the Greyhound bus in San Francisco by her irate Italian boyfriend.

Some months went by before the typescript arrived.

Attached to it was an old black-and-white photo of a ladies hockey team, signed on the back with a big heart 'Love from Natalie'. I edited the book and sent it back to her. A few weeks later she wrote saying she was working for the Leamington Spa Poetry Festival and invited me to come and do a reading. A couple of school workshops were thrown in for the following morning, which, together with the reading, would make up quite a handsome fee. I agreed to this and she wrote back saying that the Festival was putting writers up in private houses, in order to save money, and that, if it was all right with me, I would be staying with her. I wrote back saying this was all right with me.

When the time came, I set off for Leamington wearing my best shirt and feeling optimistic. To get to Leamington, you take the train from Paddington, change at Reading, then take a train north. I got out at Reading, made enquiries and got on the next train to Lymington on the south coast. (I found out later that this is where you take the ferry to the Isle of Wight.) Realizing what I had done, I ran up and down the compartment like a trapped animal, asking people whether I should get out at the next stop, or stay on the train to Lymington and start again from there. Opinion seemed to suggest that I should stay on the train. So it was that I arrived at Lymington just as my audience were taking their seats for my reading at Leamington. Instead of amusing them with stories of mishaps in the States, it seemed I was off gathering material nearer home.

I rang Natalie on her mobile, explaining what had happened. She said not to worry, jump on the next train and she'd keep the audience happy. I changed trains at Reading again and arrived at Leamington Library exactly three hours late for my reading. Natalie was waiting in the entrance for me – a pretty graduate student on work experience.

The audience was sizeable and everyone was very nice about the long 'intermission', during which they were afraid to say they'd made a start on the wine and nibbles. Natalie whisked me to the podium and I began the difficult task of being worth waiting three hours for. Almost as soon as I started it became apparent that this was not going to be possible. Within a minute, the audience were shuffling their feet, as if they were getting ready to leave. Although they had been able to control themselves, even enjoy themselves, while sitting there doing nothing, to have this feat capped by a reading was too much for them. I understood how they felt. I apologized once more and asked if I could buy anyone a drink. As I descended from the podium, Natalie approached, saying what a valiant job I'd done and would I mind signing a few copies of my book. Not a trace of dismay, or even surprise, showed on my face as she introduced me to her parents, in whose house I was going to be staying. They were teachers at the school where I was going to be taking the workshops next morning, so they could take me there in their car. I expressed my delight with these arrangements.

There were one or two copies of my libidinous travel book to sign, then it was a short walk to where I would be staying. As we left the library I found myself walking with Natalie's mother, who, to my alarm, was holding a copy of the incriminating item in her hand. She told me how much she'd enjoyed the reading and how pleased they were that I was going to be staying with them in their spare room. Looking me in the eye and with almost no hint of irony in her voice, she added, 'I've read your book.'

'Every library should try to be complete on something, if it were only the history of pinheads.' Oliver Wendell Holmes

Elizabeth McCracken

Let's just say I deserved it. I had angered the Gods of Mortification through hubris: I had mortified another writer, my friend Ann Patchett. My mortification of Ann was unsubtle and entirely accidental, without nuance, without evil, and the Gods of Mortification looked down upon me and clucked their terrible, humiliating, lemon-meringue-pie-to-the-face tongues, and decided to show me how it was done.

It started like this: Ann and I sometimes do a dog and pony show at public libraries in the US. We stand at a podium and argue about who's the dog and who's the pony, and it's much easier than appearing alone and we get to go on trips together and it's all very fine. Ann is better at most things than I am, and so she usually negotiates the fee: I'm liable to agree to read for a pat on the back and unlimited use of the library's ladies' room. Last year I got an e-mail from a library inviting us to come. So I asked Ann, and she said it sounded great, and I passed along the contact information.

Or so I thought.

Turns out I had received two invitations to read: one for Ann and me, and one for me alone. I had passed along the information from the second library. Happily, Ann was laughing when she called me to say that I owed her big: they'd agreed on a fee, and then Ann gave *her* travel information as well, and the librarian was confused. 'You don't want both of us?' asked Ann. Well, said the librarian, she couldn't pay Ann an honorarium, and she couldn't pay for Ann's travel, and, moreover, she really hadn't planned on Ann reading at the library, but if Ann wanted to come with me and share my hotel room, she was more than welcome. If it was all right with me, of course. She'd have to ask my permission.

You see how I had it coming.

Flash forward a few months. I fly to Florida and check into that selfsame hotel. It's on the interstate, with a window that, the desk clerk has told me, looks onto the pool. Actually, it looks onto a wall; the pool is merely audible (children cannonballing into it, children screaming). It is conveniently located next to two other motels, and exactly nothing else, and so I have to wait for a librarian – different from the one who'd invited me, who was on vacation – to pick me up. But she does and she's charming and doesn't blink when I say I need to have two glasses of white wine before I read to calm my nerves, she just takes me to a bar.

The library is very nice, too.

When I walk into the auditorium, I am met by a man who tells me his name is Ed. He tells me his name is Ed in such a confidential tone, while shaking my hand, that I wonder whether he has ever before broken down and confessed to anyone that his name is Ed. Ed has teeth like flying buttresses, sandy brown. He tells me he's awfully glad to meet me, he likes to meet all the authors, he hasn't read my books but he's hoping that the librarian will allow him to take away the photo of me that is now resting on the easel by the auditorium door. He wants me to sign it. He wants to compile a book of all the pictures of all the authors who ever read at this public library, starting with me. 'I want that picture,' he says, looking at my picture. Then we are mercifully interrupted.

'Ed, leave her alone,' says a dour woman. She is short and plump and wearing stiff blue shorts that show off her skinny calves. The shorts are so immense, and so stiff, and Ed's teeth so very like flying buttresses, that she appears to be waiting for Quasimodo to swing by and ring her.

'I'm just talking!' says Ed.

'Can't you see she wants to talk to her fans? I'm Ed's wife,' she confesses to me.

It's true: I do want to talk to my fans. I try to adopt a look of modesty and approachability, and scan the auditorium to see: Ed, his wife, the librarian. I shake all of their hands again.

Eventually a few more people show up, though not enough to justify the generous fee that Patchett has negotiated. Still, there's one nice little old lady in the audience, wearing a strange plastic brace around her torso. I assume it's meant to straighten out an osteoporotic back. I give her a comforting smile, and she returns it. Most readers know the comfort of picking out an attentive, cheerful audience member to calm their nerves, especially if the crowd is small. She'll do.

I read just a little, and then I talk about my writing. Look, I'm right: there's Grandma in the front row, nodding and smiling. She looks like she's having the time of her life. I'm probably her favourite author! This is probably a big thrill! She can't get enough of me! What a fool I was! What a poor, sad, sick, pathetic fool!

'And sometimes I just indulge myself,' I say about my own

writing process, and Grandma calls out, 'Those must have been the times when I had trouble.'

'Oh?' I say brightly.

She says, 'Yes. I read your short stories, and sometimes, I just couldn't understand them.'

Make no mistake: the Gods of Mortification recognize false modesty. I should have said, 'Gosh, too bad, sister. Maybe if you take a night course you could become halfway literate, and then you wouldn't stumble over perfectly straightforward English.'

Instead, I deliver a fine speech about how every short story is a collaboration between writer and reader, and every reading of a short story is valid, and how I was sorry that she didn't enjoy them but that didn't mean that there was anything wrong with her reading of them–'

'I know!' she says excitedly. 'I mean, I'd get to the end of a story, and I'd say to myself, what was the point of that?'

I nod.

'That was a complete waste of time!' she says. 'I mean, really, every single story, I thought–'

I nod again.

'That was the dumbest thing I ever read!' she says.

'I'm going to crawl under the podium now,' I say, and briefly, and literally, I do.

When I resurface, she has her hand up again, but so does an overtan, unwashed man sitting at the back who has the square head and tiny mouth of a police sketch.

'I have an easy three-part question,' he says.

'Shoot,' I tell him. I mean it literally, but unfortunately he seems to be unarmed.

'One: will you be offended if I leave in three minutes? Two: are you married? Three: is it all right if I write to you?'

'Um,' I say. 'One: no. Two: um. Three: well, OK.'

'Thank you,' he says in a meaningful way, like an anchorman signing off for the night, and he gets up and leaves two and a half full minutes before his deadline, and doesn't ask for an address, leaving me to assume he will contact me by astral projection.

I answer a few more questions wearily, and then sit down next to a pile of more books than there are people in the room, and offer to sign books.

'You hate me!' says Grandma, who of course is first in line. She is clutching her copy of my short stories to the spot of her plastic brace that would shield her heart, if she had one. I want to snatch my book away from her and dandle it on my knee and stroke its pages in a comforting way; I certainly do not write my name on the title page and give it back. 'You *hate* me!' she repeats.

'I don't *hate* you,' I say. I could break her wrist with a handshake, if I wanted, and I do, but she doesn't offer.

'No, you *hate* me,' she says ecstatically. 'But you know, I read your last book, too, and actually I enjoyed it. Although the second chapter–'

'Shut the fuck up, lady,' I say, or words to that effect.

I sign a few more books, and then everyone has gone, except Ed and his wife. They look beautiful to me now. They have not read my books and therefore have no opinions. They believe I have fans.

'You're funny,' says the wife mournfully.

'Thank you,' I answer.

'You know what you should write?' she says. She stands at the podium and looks out over the now empty folding chairs of the auditorium. 'A book about the lighter side of losing a child.'

'I beg your pardon?' I ask. Surely I've misunderstood the question.

'You know. Finding the humour in a child's death. Like a jokebook.'

'There's humour in it?' I ask.

'Oh, yes,' she says, in a voice that suggests there is not a lighter side of a single moment on this earth. 'Oh, of course. My son died.'

I nod.

She still isn't looking at me. She's looking at the long-gone audience.

'And you know, one day, Ed and I were standing on the beach. Ed was eating a Subway sub. You know? And this seagull came down, and he stole it out of Ed's hand. We knew it was my son. He'd taken the form of a seagull. My son loved ham and cheese. And Ed was jumping up and down and yelling at the seagull. And *it was funny*,' she says, the way small children say *The End* when they finish telling a made-up nonsensical story, because there's no other way to tell.

'Oh,' I say. 'I'm so sorry.'

'A book like that,' she says flatly. 'It would be a big hit. You could go on Rosie O'Donnell. It's *needed*.'

'All right,' I tell her. 'I'll think about it.'

And so I left without even being able to feel sorry for myself. On the bright side, Patchett felt a hell of a lot better.

'Their tricks and craft hae put me daft,
They've ta'en me in and a' that,
But clear your decks, and Here's the sex!
I like the jads for a' that.'
Robert Burns, 'The Jolly Beggars'

Louis de Bernières

A few years ago I went to Perth, Western Australia, to partici-
pate in the literature festival, and for the most part had a
wonderful time, especially as part of the deal was to go to
Karratha and Broome to do literary events. In Broome, a tropical paradise, I went fishing in an alligator swamp, and had
the misfortune to run over a wallaby. In Karratha, a mining
town set in a landscape from Mars, I had to do the first-ever
literary event. It was co-hosted by the Rotarians and the Sorop-
timists, and we had to approve their minutes before my reading could actually begin. I later discovered that the latter were
locally referred to as the Soropticows. Driving around the
countryside the next day, I came across the bronze monument
to Red Dog that would eventually lead to my eponymous
small book.

In Perth, one of my duties was to appear on panels. I don't
often do this any more, as I am fed up with hearing myself
and other writers bullshitting fluently and speciously about
whatever topics the audiences care to raise. In France the cult

of the literary intellectual is farcically out of control, and I would hate to be part of any such tendency in the Anglophone world. There is, after all, no reason for a writer's opinions to be thought superior to anyone else's, and you might as well have a panel of my dad, the vet, the tobacconist, and the two fat people from the St John Ambulance Brigade who usually sit at the back of the audience.

I was still fresh in the wake of Captain Gorilla's Mandarin, and so was the natural choice for a panel about love. I never claimed to be brilliant at it, or particularly knowledgeable about it; it was enough that I had created characters who could do it. Out in the sparkling sunshine, seated at a long table overlooking a crowd of expectant Australians, I found myself improvising opinions that sounded worryingly like those of my mother.

I can no longer recall who the other members of the panel were, but one of them was a bright young Aussie, whose gimmick for the day was to bring along an S&M prostitute. This formidable lady was nearly young, and was built like the proverbial brick shithouse. She was adorned with much colourful warpaint, and she wore the standard-issue stiletto boots, black fishnet stockings, and that odd scarlet garment which is half frilly swimming-costume and half corset. One look confirmed that in the unlikely event of there ever being a sexual encounter between us, it would have to be she who coughed up the wherewithal.

She took over the entire event. Cracking her whip, she commanded the audience to stand up, sit down, stand up, bow down. The respectable, mainly middle-aged and elderly Aussie audience meekly obeyed, and I suddenly realized why it had been so easy to get the Anzacs to commit suicide at Gallipoli.

These antics naturally made our panel ridiculous. My irritation caused me to suffer a fit of pedantry, because the panel was supposed to be about love, and I couldn't see what S&M prostitution had to do with it. Sounding ever more like my mother I tried to make the distinction between love and sex, and found the audience agreeing with me vigorously. Everyone knows, after all, that the best sex arises out of emotional connection. Even so, for a long time afterwards I felt embarrassed by the whole thing. The event, however spurious, had been sabotaged, the audience had been humiliated, and I came out of it feeling that I had exposed myself as pompous and puritanical.

'There is nothing more dreadful to an author than neglect, compared with which, reproach, hatred and opposition are names of happiness.' Samuel Johnson

John Banville

It was a cold March in North America, and I was on a publicity tour: ten cities in eleven days: the usual. I was midway through the trip when my publishers suggested I might like to make a detour to Florida, to read at a book festival there. Why not? Another day, another city.

I arrived in Miami on an afternoon such as I thought might only be experienced in Araby, everything in burnous white and limitless gradations of soft ochre and pale blue. Seen from the airport road, the city shimmered in a violet haze, its silver-and-glass towers trembling. My hotel, on South Beach, faced a purplish sea. On the sand a rout of sun-bronzed gods and honeyed maenads mellowly romped, all of them naked except for the odd strip of candy-bright cloth applied here and there to their perfect persons. The hotel itself seemed to date from the 1930s – big wooden ceiling-fans lazily turning, jalousie shutters on the windows, a walnut-panelled bar – but later I learned that the place had been distressed to make it look old. 'Distressed' in this usage was new to me; so were roller-blades.

Between the beach and the road there was a palm-lined pedestrian way, where more glistening, chocolate-skinned giants swirled and spun as if on air. I stood at the window and looked down upon this bright scene of prelapsarian play and thought I might have landed on another, infinitely finer planet, than the one, off on the other side of the galaxy, upon which the world as I know it was hamfistedly modelled.

I went for a walk. That was a mistake. All the clothes I had brought with me were fit only for winter weather. The spectacle of a tweed-clad, pale, perspiring dwarf staggering amongst them must have amused the South Beachers, those lordly inhabitants of the planet Miami. I fled to the safe distress of my hotel room, where I lay on the bed through the rest of the long afternoon. The fan circled above me. The sun fell slowly down the sky. The liquid hissing of the air conditioner seemed the sound of time itself trying not to pass.

The reading took place next day in a large, glass-walled auditorium with the acoustics of an echo-chamber. On the stage along with me was a chap who the previous day had been awarded the Pulitzer Prize. There was a large audience, all of whom, I felt sure, had come to hear him, and for that thrill were sullenly willing to put up with me. After the reading, of which I remember nothing, there was the book signing. This took place in a wide, sunny plaza that made me think of an execution yard in some South American republic of drugs and banditry. Against one wall – there could have been bullet marks, there could have been bloodstains – two small tables stood, piled with books, the Pulitzer laureate's, and mine. He had a queue of excited autograph hunters that stretched halfway up the spine of Florida; I had three customers, or so I thought, one of them an academic who had written on my work, the second of whom looked decidedly unhinged, and the third a kindly fellow who stepped up first and leaned forward confidentially and, with a smile that was nothing but tender, whispered to me a sentence I often hear, even yet, in my dreams. 'I'm not going to buy a book,' he confided, 'but you looked so lonely there, I thought I'd come and talk to you.'

'Other people's eggs have two yolks.' Bulgarian proverb

Don Paterson

After some unspeakable business at Goole Arts Centre, we head for what the promoter proudly introduces as 'the best restaurant in Goole'. I default to the chicken bhuna, which turns out to be a kind of artificial mycelium woven into a chicken effect and drowned in luminous chemicals. Throughout the meal the promoter recites his own poems from memory. I return to the digs. In the hotel bar the wall-eyed landlord carefully inscribes a perfect arse in the foam of my Guinness, which promptly evaporates before my eyes. I retire to a tiny bare room built around an irregular nonagon, or rather accidentally formed by the unequal pressure of several other rooms; through one of the many walls a couple, possibly human, are making love, though it sounds more like someone is killing them with alternate blows. I attempt to make a cup of tea. The two tiny UHT individual milk-pots are both sour. I hear a low and long intestinal gurgle, the sort of sound that heralds the onset of tropical giardia. I assume it is coming from me, but then the plug pops out of the little washhand basin and raw sewage foams up to form a little pulsing brown wellhead, and the room quickly fills with the smell of hydrogen sulphide and death.

A recurring dream. Hours of inaccurate Pali chanting and 150cc of Macallan concealed in a Volvic bottle finally sees one of the hell-planes of my nightmares (the DC 10 with its bolt-on engines; the lopsided Fokker 50) dump me unceremoniously on the ground again. The heat or the cold slams into me like a door, and I stagger down the steps onto the melting or icebound tarmac. I pass through customs as through the lower bardos, and am led to the waiting car by the gentle psychopomps of the British Council, as a man to his doom, which always takes the image of himself, *of his own book.*

Exeter. After a tolerable meal of egg and broccoli quiche and beansprout salad in the cafe – there being no meat alternative – my friend Michael Donaghy and I do the reading. We also throw in a little music. Mildly euphoric after an evening which contained no major disasters, we retire to the dressing room. Michael produces two bodhrans, an instrument for which I have no gift, but an obscure and persistent enthusiasm. Iron John was heavy in the air that year, and we drum and sweat a whole bunch in our vests. We lose track of the time. We walk to the digs. The building is in darkness. We have no key. No amount of ringing and banging will raise the landlady. We return to the venue, which is now also in darkness. We resign ourselves to a night in the car. It is now bitterly cold, and ice is forming on the windows. We find one tiny tartan blanket in the boot. We try to sleep, but the beansprouts are starting to talk – for me, at least, the promotion of raw vegetables beyond their decorative role is something of a novelty.

At least, MD philosophically observes, these eruptions have the effect of raising the temperature briefly; but since opening the window is not an option, the trade-off eventually proves too difficult to stomach. Heartily sick of each other, we separate at 5 a.m. I leave for the station to wait two hours for the nine-hour journey home, while MD heads off, I vividly recall, for no reason – to Redcar. I sit on the freezing platform and watch the dawn spread in the east, like blood beneath a shirt.

I have been booked to address the Penang Poetry Society on Open Mic Night. I am playing music elsewhere in the country (a tour that will culminate in a concert in the Bornean rainforest, where we will be met with a silence beyond mere human indifference: the *whole Earth* fell silent, as it did for Orpheus. As our last number died away I heard only the cry of a rabid monkey fifty miles upriver, the dead thump of a falling breadfruit.) A Malaysian lady, spotting the bodhran – the bodhran, the last refuge of the charlatan, the instrument which should always stay at home – insists that I accompany her reading. She clicks her fingers to give me the tempo. I lay down an acceptable 4/4 shuffle with a hint of a backstick. She looks at me with a kind of blank contempt. Then she closes her eyes, composes herself, and begins to shout. *'Fred's dead/ in his bed/hit his head/in the shed/then he bled/got all red/in the shed/Fred's dead . . .'*

At the interval I leave the superchilled striplit room, and go outside to try and revive my circulation in the hot night. Moths the size of giant pigeons are swarming under the palms. One lumbers towards me. I think, for some reason, of the little cabbage-white alighting on the racket of the young and shyly pretty Chris Evert at Wimbledon, and how the whole game stopped while its tiny blessing was conferred. I realize I cannot open the doors of the venue to get back inside. I start thumping on them frantically. The giant moths start to dive-bomb my head. On their backs they carry the faces of demons.

Soiled underwear in the guest bed is a popular motif in reading stories. In the long years before they learned to say *No* to all offers of 'hospitality', most writers will have encountered this at least once, especially when the bed has been vacated by the host. Though once, in a hotel in Telford, I found some red silk thongs under the pillow, rolled into a little torus; I found this rather touching – it was almost as if they had been left there as part of the turndown service, along with *A Belgian Chocolate For Your Dreams*. But experience means you no longer dare stretch your toes near the very foot of the bed, where the grubby Ys and jockeys hastily discarded in passion are most likely to be wedged. Nothing, though, could have prepared me for the cardboard-stiff 'special pants' I once found jammed under the headboard of my student host.

We are often put up in children's bedrooms; I have frequently woken crapulously to ant-farms and terrifying ranks of My Little Ponies, and more than once to the ejected child standing silently above me at 6.30 a.m., their expression balefully fixed on the very old and ugly Goldilocks before them. The Worst Bed was in Wivenhoe: a shapeless, single fold-down foam chair lined with a kind of 70s olive-black fake newt-skin. I was so exhausted after my long journey I would happily have fallen into it, though, had it not been in the centre of a living room where the organizer had thoughtfully decided to throw a party for his students. I finally crawled into it at 4 a.m. and woke three hours later, my skin stuck everywhere to its plastic hide with beer and vodka, and my hair full of ash.

*   *   *

Weeks spent in a van full of other men – where the social highlight of the month has been a brief encounter with a Hilton hand-towel – can leave you, like, in a really bad way, man. Hence most itinerant male musicians' familiarity with that early-morning manoeuvre known as 'coyote arm', named for that most pragmatic of animals, who will gnaw off a limb to free itself from a snare. I suspect, though, that there are far more one-armed women walking the streets: confused and disarmed by the magical fug of smoke and candlelight, they have mistaken the saxophonist's fluent choruses for conversational urbanity and his suit for linen, only to wake beside a drooling and twitching beast identical to the one she has left at home. I've been lucky in the friends I've found on the road. I have never had the experience, as others have had, of retiring with a lady who turned out not to be, or being talked into wearing a gimp suit, or being introduced to the husband upon arrival at the flat (*cheerfully*), or suddenly realizing that my partner's wild orgasm was in fact a *grand mal* seizure. But the contract between such international lovers always states that you must never meet again. It is an understanding both parties must honour. (Dishonesty in this regard is a Very Bad Thing – for either party. Musicians, remarkably, get hurt too.)

I was back in an East European town I never thought I would see again. Last time, I had given a reading there; this time I was back, guitar in hand, for the annual Jazz Festival. I was already badly bruised from a kind of Oedipal showdown: I was supporting an American guitarist called Ralph Towner, a musician from whom I have derived my entire playing style, and a guitarist so wholly superior to me in every department I can barely claim to play the same instrument. I was positively eviscerated by the experience, and hit the bar.

And heavens, there she was again, that pale, pale face . . .

Oh. She was with the Americans. Worse – I quickly registered – with the bass player. Bassists are the fastest workers in the ensemble. As everyone knows, all jazz musicians play with a deeply pained Jazz Face. (For the record, this look is 3% affectation and 97% concentration: jazz is a tightrope with absurdity on one side, and disgrace on the other.) True, the sound the bassist produces often resembles a series of low raspberries, but because of the beautiful big instrument he wrestles it from, he is the only musician whose Jazz Face looks like lovemaking. This is a fine way of advertising yourself. Compared with the rest of the band – who appear to be flailing around in a welter of agonized constipation, memory loss and recent bereavement – he always presents a figure of attractive self-possession.

The bassist was obviously relating some incident that had happened onstage that night. She threw her head back and laughed her laugh, that perfect little staccato arpeggio, three ascending fifths ending in a squeal; she had one white arm held out before her, and the other raised above her head, like a flamenco dancer. I realized she was cradling an imaginary bass, fingering – *uh* – its imaginary headstock. I approached her. She'd obviously missed my set, and had no idea I was in town; she looked at me with that vague repulsion you feel when you encounter a thing in the wrong element: a fish on a lawn, a bird on the road, a fully-dressed man face-down in a swimming pool. We talked, while the bassist looked on with a perfect expressionlessness. (Very clever. This is how you play this one: *you shut down your aura.*) I addressed her by the shortened form of her name he had yet to learn; I reminded her of a joke we'd shared, which we clearly no longer did; I even – all fake-innocent, but cruelly, unforgivably – asked who was looking after her child that evening. I took the hint. I somehow managed to effect a slow dematerialization, and reappeared like a spectre at the bar again. From there I watched the whole lovely negotiation; I couldn't hear a word, but knew it well enough. *Look. Bottom line. I go to Padua tomorrow, Stockholm Sunday, back to Chicago Monday morning. You and me both know there's more chance of lightning hitting us now than us two ever* . . . and so on, until . . . *but we've got tonight.* Then her even more lovely mock-disbelief, amused shrug, coy acquiescence. They disappeared into the dressing room and emerged fifty minutes later (reader, I counted them; by then all that was left to me was to make a masochistic fetish of my solitude). They stopped on the stairs, and he turned to her and took her face in both hands, and muttered some poignant sincerity – for only fools and those who have never known the road believe these liaisons are unbeautiful and insincere – and they left together for the hotel.

'Humour is the first of the gifts to perish in a foreign tongue.'
Virginia Woolf

Michael Holroyd

Seldom have I written an essay feeling so spoilt for choice. Which episode, from a career glittering with mortifications, shall I choose? Should it, for example, be my first literary lunch? The other speaker was Harry Secombe. He had written a serious book and wished to speak seriously about it. I had also written what I hoped was a serious book, a serious comedy of manners, and wanted to make some jokes. But his reputation as a famous 'Goon', and the description of me as a literary biographer, completely prevented us from doing what we wanted. When Harry Secombe rose to his feet and said 'Good afternoon', people fell off their chairs with laughter and rolled around in ecstasy; while I, firing off some jokes, saw the same audience frown learnedly and begin making notes on their menus. It was a fiasco, and we agreed afterwards that we should have swapped speeches.

Worse than this was my first literary festival, the Bedford Square Book Bang. I hadn't been asked to do anything very difficult – simply stand in the rain next to a wheelbarrow full

of books and sign all those that were bought. The trouble
was that none was being bought. Seeing me standing damply
there, like an unemployed gardener, my publisher comman-
deered a megaphone and bellowed out the news that 'the
famous biographer' was even now signing copies of his book.
'Roll up!' he cried – and suddenly out of the gloom someone
did roll up. He was carrying a copy of my book which, he
explained, he would like to return as not being worth the
paper it was written on – an insult that, as the rain fell on its
pages, swelling and distorting them visibly, was much magni-
fied. A scuffle developed during which, I like to think, I
inserted my blurred name. But in the end I sold minus one
copy – a score that should surely earn me an entry in *The
Guinness Book of Records*.

But perhaps it is wiser to choose an overseas humiliation,
such as the time I gave a lecture in a very large, totally empty
hall in the United States. 'We'll wait a little for stragglers,' said
the polite professor who was to introduce me. We waited but
no one straggled. Eventually we clambered on to the stage
and the professor introduced me in glowing language – I only
wish someone had been there to hear him. It seemed he was
too paralysed by embarrassment to call off the event, and I,
needing the cheque, was obliged to deliver my lecture, speaking for forty minutes into the thin air. Halfway through this
performance someone came through the door, stopped and
stood staring at us. Was this surreal soliloquy a rehearsal for
something? I turned to him and, like the Ancient Mariner,
tried to hold him there. But with a look of alarm he turned
on his heel (a movement I had read about but never seen
before) and ran out. I felt exhausted by the time I finished
speaking, and, there being no questions, the professor rose
and thanked me. As we climbed off the podium together, he

remarked without, so far as I could tell, any trace of irony: 'Your lecture would have gone down even better, Mr Holroyd, with a larger audience.' I consoled myself with the thought that there had been an audience of two: us two. Later I heard that there was a students' uprising that day, sounds of which – a muffled chanting – had wafted through the hall, accompanying me as I stood mouthing my words.

Irony, I have discovered, is often a good defence against mortification, but sometimes it can backfire, especially when you are abroad. A prime example of this happened to me in Moscow where I went as a member of a GB/USSR conference of writers. We fielded a distinguished team: Matthew Evans (now Lord Evans), Melvyn Bragg (now Lord Bragg), my wife Margaret Drabble, Francis King, Penelope Lively, Fay Weldon and myself. These were pre-Gorbachev days and the Soviet team of writers seemed to us old and dour. When it was the turn of one of us to speak, they would put their feet on the table, read their newspapers, and tell each other incomprehensible jokes. I was scheduled to speak on the last morning and, angered by what I had witnessed, I rewrote my speech and gave a copy to the simultaneous translator. I spoke slowly, with withering scorn, even contempt, and was gratified to see that I was getting the full attention of the Soviet team. They put down their feet and their newspapers, ceased joking and listened attentively. Much encouraged, I assumed my most acid tone, piling one ingenious insult upon another, building up a Gothic edifice of cunning invective. My final crescendo of abuse was greeted with loud applause, and one of our team passed me a brief note: 'Does irony translate?' Evidently mine did not, and what left me as subtle and devastating satire arrived at the other side of the table as a peculiarly sophisticated hymn of praise.

The afternoon sessions of our conference were jollier affairs, largely because of the excellent lunches which featured many simultaneously translated, simultaneously drunk, toasts. I drank for England that week and often appeared at breakfast wearing dark glasses. At lunch, on the final day, much to Maggie's embarrassment, I rose swaying to my feet and raising my glass high (before attempting to smash it to the floor over my shoulder) proposed a toast to the great spirit that had brought us, and our literature, together – 'the spirit of vodka!'

Maggie said she would never take me anywhere again. But occasionally she relents and I am able to send her children evidence of some fresh mortification – such as the photograph of us before dawn in Ireland, in front of the cream of Irish literature, singing along with that notorious pop group, the Dubliners.

Sean O'Reilly

. . . There was that party remember. She wanted it. She wanted me. I was sure she did, she told me once, no she didn't. I was younger then, believed in everything just in case. She was tormenting me but if I had reported her to the authorities she would have denied it to the death, that was the type of her, she didn't know what she wanted you see, she was in conflict with her own desires. I wasn't. I was free. It was the mushroom season. The world was dank. The way she looked at me blinking with surprise like she had forgotten my presence was the perfect camouflage for her hunger or the way she opened one eye, the bigger eye, the brows didn't match either, that sly bit wider when she spoke to me and laughed at the institutional egg-box ceiling when I couldn't find the words to answer and glared at her, the strangest laugh I had ever heard, a gurgle at the back of her throat culminating in a hoarse splutter through her lips – it was all typical of a woman repressing her deeper instincts. She was driving me mad. With her fucken theory about Mrs Radcliffe and de Sade and *Les Crimes de*

l'Amour and her cowboy boots and her plastic toadstool rings
and she never had a pen for she liked to give the impression
of spontaneity and eccentric inspirations. She had it all worked
out. She devoted the beginning of every class, no, seminar was
the new institutional egg-box word, to testing the various pens
offered by her assembled slaves, the Apostate Queen, putting
her name to the order for the brutal rape and execution of a
hundred virgins, this kind of innocence must be stamped out.
I never offered her mine, my pen I mean, innocence had not
yet sprouted in me, and she was wise to my rebellion, that's
what the whole show was about every week, to see whether
I would succumb. Even so it was the only seminar I went to.
For three hours every week I sat in Gothic Literature and
listened to the stories of sex-fiend monks and randy nuns and
diabolical confessions from her big toothy mouth. She had
freckles on her teeth. Her tongue was undersized. I was beginning to understand that there were types of violence I had
never dreamed of. I was on edge permanently. The mushies
were out, did I mention that? People were disappearing. The
bars were empty or the next minute incredibly vicious. One
day in class I saw her nipples growing and growing and they
were about to tell me to do something only I got out the door in
time. She came straight after me into the corridor. She started
unbuttoning her shirt. This is what you want isn't it, she said.
No she fucken didn't. I was ordered into her office. Then she
lay across the desk and pulled up her long denim skirt. Like
fuck she did. I got a mouthful about my behaviour, my bad
confrontational attitude. I knew it was code. She was really
saying that she couldn't, it was too risky, maybe after I gradu-
ated. I played along with her; I was able to grasp the real truth
behind her words. We had to wait for the right moment. Then
there was that party at her house for some visiting writer, a

bloody poet. I only went because I could tell she wanted me to be there. I'd been on the go for a few days before it. My piss had turned black with fungal ink. I remember when I went into the house that the stairs were too narrow for even my finger to get up to the bathroom. She was talking to the poet in the kitchen, drinking punch. She was barefoot. Artfully, she showed some uncertainty about my name. Then she asked me if it was raining. I had no idea. But you're soaking wet, she said with a weird look to the malevolent scheming poet. That's when I understood. The back door was open: I fought my way through its emptiness. In the garden I started searching, in the bushes, under a wheelbarrow, down on my knees sweeping the leaves away. Luckily there wasn't a shed or I might have been there all night. I studied the arrangement of the pegs on the clothes line for a sign. Eventually I found it. She had left me a message under a stone which commanded me to hide in her bedroom before everyone left. I decided to stay outside and prepare myself, cleanse my mind, in the rain, a delicious misty rain. The Queen had chosen her mate for the night. My time had come. My people looked to me in dread and awe. Then I saw the lights go off in the house. I went back in. I must have been surprised to find so many people still there. It wasn't particularly dark either. I was already naked to the waist, an agaric warrior, rained on, maybe a bit mucky. The guests stared. Halfway up the stairs I stopped and looked down. They were gathering in the hall to behold me. Some of them were shouting at me: one man with horns attempted to grab hold of me and I swung my boot at him. This ugly rabble were nothing more than shadows, figments, the exteriorization of my guilt which she had shown me must be confronted and eradicated. This was the test, I was telling myself, I have to show her that I have courage, that I am a man. I began to take off my trousers. There she was now herself among them, the sarcastic poet beside her, screaming at me to get out of her house forthwith. But that's how she had to play it, this was part of the foul phantasmagoria to be fought through. I had my cock out in my hands by this stage. I held it up against them like a crucifix. The demons shrieked with horror. The poet smirked: it was all going according to plan. Then I ran for her bedroom, held the door shut behind me. There was a big bed with a red eiderdown, unmade. The pillows were lilac and the size of sheep. I had never seen anything so beautiful. My whole life made sense. The ghouls were whispering through the door. They were talking about the police, the fucken spoil-sport squad. I heard sirens but it might have been the souls in the underworld calling to me not to give in. You can imagine the rest. But if you can't be bothered then let's just say they must have decided to leave me alone to calm down and I must have got under the Eider-down of Bliss and passed out. When I opened my eyes, my girlfriend of the time was sneering down at me with a kind of disgust that should never have been made known to her. Her face would never look the same again. Not that I saw much of it. The only other person in the room was the poet lurking in the corner with my clothes in her hands. The Queen was nowhere to be seen as I was led out of the house into my girlfriend's car. They must have called her to come and get me. I sat in the back seat of course. It was still dark. The streets were as empty as I was. My girlfriend bent the rear view mirror so that she wouldn't have to look at me. Neither of us spoke. I had the feeling something momentous had happened. I'm sorry, I said when we stopped outside my flat. She told me to fuck off and drove away to another life. The university were informed of course. I was not allowed to continue with my studies in Gothic literature. They were going to throw me out altogether but for some mysterious reason I was reprieved under condition I attended counselling three times a week. The counsellor was gorgeous. She was lonely. She was dying for it, I could see it in her eyes. We went for walks together in the woods. No we didn't.

'We must travel in the direction of our fear.' John Berryman

Charles Simic

One night in New York, it was so hot and humid in a bookstore where I was reading my poems, I was soaked with sweat, my pants kept sliding down, so I had to constantly pull them up with one hand while I held the book in the other. A fellow I knew told me afterwards that he was enthralled. He and his companion were sure I'd forget for a moment and let them fall down. Another time in Monterey, California, I was reading in a nearly empty auditorium of the local college adjoining one in which the movie *King Kong* was being shown to a packed audience. At one point, during one of my most lyrical love poems, I could hear the great ape growl behind my back as he was on his way to strangle me. Back in the 1960s, in some youth centre in some miserable little town on Long Island, I was put on the programme between an amateur magician and a fellow who was a mind-reader and the audience of local punks was not told who I was and what I was supposed to be doing. I recall their bewildered expressions as I was reading my first poem. In Detroit, I had a baby howl while I read and then a lapdog someone had sneaked in started to yelp. I was so drunk in Geneva, New York, I demanded that all the lights be turned off except the one on my lectern, and then I proceeded to read for two hours, some of the poems twice, as I was told the next day. In the 1970s, after hearing my poem 'Breasts', a dozen women walked out in Oberlin, Ohio, each one slamming the door behind her. In a high school in Medford, Oregon I was introduced as the world-famous mystery writer, Bernard Zimic. In San Jose, I lost the fellow I was supposed to be following in my car at the peak of the rush-hour traffic and realized I had no idea where the reading was. I drove ahead thinking he would notice I'm not behind him and stop by the side of the road. I went past all the downtown and suburban exits and finally figured the hell with him, I'm going home to San Francisco. Since I had to go back the way I came from, I decided on the spur of the moment to take one of the exits and ask, except there was no one to ask at eight in the evening in a neighbourhood of small apartment houses and tree-lined streets. After circling for a while, I saw an old Chinese man walking alone. I stopped the car and asked him, very conscious of how ridiculous I was, did he happen to know of a poetry reading? Yes, he said, in the church around the corner. In Aurora, New York on beautiful Lake Geneva I gave the shortest reading ever. It lasted exactly twenty-eight minutes, whereas the crowd and the organizers expected a full hour. I had an excellent excuse, however. I squeezed the reading between the first and final quarter of an NBA playoff game and ran back to my motel outracing a couple of women who wanted me to sign books. In Ohrid, Macedonia I read into a dead mike to an audience of thousands who would not have understood me even if they had heard me, but who nevertheless applauded after every poem. Now, I ask you, how much more can one ask from life?

'It's the admirer and the watcher who provoke us to all the insanities we commit.' Seneca

A. L. Kennedy

Literary gatherings are, of course, to be avoided for many reasons: people asking who you are in the polite expectation that they will have heard of you – they won't – while others engage you with enthusiastic praise, having mistaken you for someone whose work they admire and you freeze behind the ghastly smile of a trapped iguana. It is equally possible (if you're me) to spend an entire evening lavishly complimenting a Great Man who turns out to be another Great Man entirely – although enthusiasm always renders me incoherent, so I may have got away with that one. Beyond these minor troubles, I would also not advise wearing black trousers and then sitting carelessly on white patio furniture – this may lead to your spending the rest of the evening at a distressingly A-List affair (your invite being due to typing error) wandering about with white stripes across your arse and thighs which nobody mentions until you get home and are then more than able to point them out to yourself.

Writers' trousers are famously unpredictable in many ways,

but I haven't met another author whose trousers simply disintegrated en route to a reading. There I was, young and nervous and not wearing a frock due to poor body image issues, stuck on a late afternoon train to Edinburgh, leafing through my notes in a preparatory way and yet also feeling, somehow, chilly. After a brief investigation I discovered that the outside seams of both legs were merrily falling apart and that I was not asleep and therefore would not wake up and find I didn't have to deal with this. I then participated in the perfect preparation for a gig – namely sprinting (gingerly) through Edinburgh in search of a sewing repair shop that was still open. I did, miraculously, find such a place and persuade it to stay operational while I removed my trousers and had the unparalleled joy of standing in my jacket and socks as the sewing machine chattered away and a small but interested crowd gathered outside the plate-glass window to wish me well – or certainly to wish me something.

Obviously, I am one of the many authors who should not be encountered semi-nude without prior warning. Which means that visiting the ablutions before an event should always be undertaken with great care. A Radio Three outside broadcast and a dodgy lock once combined to introduce me to an audience member rather more than we would have wished. That particular event was already going swimmingly – I am never anything other than delighted to arrive and find a poster on the door showing the other participants' names clearly printed and my own name scrawled at the bottom in biro as a late and unwilling addition. This is always a tactful way of indicating that the other twelve people they asked before you all died or went insane and they've finally settled for you, rather than an empty seat: but it was a close-run thing.

Making broadcasts of any kind is, naturally, a mistake. The

form itself can produce intense embarrassment directly: being
mocked and reviled by passers-by while just wandering about
like a tit, because shots of writers always show them just wandering about as if they have forgotten their own address. (In
France I was once actually urinated at by a standing woman
as I just wandered about.) Or the particular programme may
release immense potential for discomfort. I can personally rec-
ommend just wandering about in an Ayrshire graveyard – a
life-sized, wax, male, nude torso blazing quietly behind you.
Passing Dog Walker: 'This about Robert Burns, then?' Shame-
faced Author, 'Erm, yes.' PDW, with gentle contempt, 'BBC
Two?' SA, 'Ah, yes.' Schools broadcasts may at first appear
less perilous, but one must constantly bear in mind that they
are broadcast to schools. Therefore, for every showing, you
must expect a subsequent two-month period of shouted abuse
from all local boys under sixteen. Interestingly, the most
common and elegantly simple slur is, 'Writer!' This goes to
prove that education does work and a whole generation has
successfully learned that to call anyone a writer is a grievous
insult.

Which is why any writer in their right mind will avoid
answering the question, 'So, what do you do?' with any degree
of truthfulness. The following question will always be, 'Published?' delivered with a darkly incredulous stare and beyond
that no response will ever be believed or believable. This is
tricky, but not half as tricky as those times when you're at a
normal party, or hill-walking, or buying swedes and suddenly
find yourself subjected to the third degree. Party Guest, 'So,
where do you think the European novel is heading?' Author,
'Do you want all of those sausages?' PG, 'The standard of
spelling has just dropped and dropped, hasn't it?' Author, 'I
think I can see some pie over there.' PG, 'Modern stuff's just

crap, though, isn't it? I mean, not yours. Well, I've never read yours, actually – but it is all shit, really, don't you think?' Author, 'I have to take one of my pills now.' Better by far to claim that you are a war criminal fleeing justice, or that you rehabilitate wasps. Although it provides clean and tidy indoor work, although it allows adults to behave like children and often get away with it, although it occasionally provides a living wage, very few people – out loud, at least – will insist on being a writer.

'A half truth in argument, like a half brick, carries better.'
Stephen Leacock

Carlo Gébler

I was in my late twenties. I had published some short stories but no first novel yet. I had no girlfriend either. One afternoon the phone rang in the flat I shared with a Dutch cameraman and I answered it.

'Are you Carlo Gébler?' The speaker was a young Dubliner, her voice breathy and lovely.

'Yes.'

'I've read some of your stories,' she said. Her name was Olivia, she added.

No sooner had I got her name but an image of Olivia was cast up before my mind's eye. She was a Celtic Charlotte Rampling, tall and willowy and sensitive and lonely like me.

Olivia explained she was calling on behalf of the London branch of the graduate society of an Irish university. She was the new secretary.

'We meet every month,' she said. She mentioned an Irish Centre in north London. 'We always have a speaker,' she continued. 'Usually from sport or business. But I want to broaden things so I wondered, would you read a story?' Of course I would. Anything for you, Olivia, I thought. But lest I appeared eager, I asked about the evening. 'There'll be a bit of society business first and then you read for half an hour, say. Then everyone will pile into the bar. And we'll pay you too.' She mentioned a modest sum.

It was a done deal. I noted the time, place and date in my diary. We said goodbye.

Time passed, and finally what I had recklessly come to consider as the evening of my date with Olivia arrived. I dressed carefully. Assuming all the males at the meeting would be Price-Waterhouse trainees in suits, I opted for the conventionally unconventional look of leather jacket and red tie. This would impress her.

Then I went to the street and I eased myself into my car, in those days a very fogeyish 1962 Morris Oxford saloon. To avoid being seen behind the wheel I parked some way from the centre and walked the last quarter mile. The venue was a sixties monstrosity with posters of shamrocks in the windows. The bar was decorated with shillelaghs and rank with the smell of old Guinness. I hardly noticed or cared. I had eyes only for O. But striding across the vomit-crusted carpet, I was appalled to see that the figure gliding towards me with shining knees and bobbed hair, was less than five foot high. It couldn't be, could it?

'You must be Carlo,' said the throaty voice. Oh yes, it was Olivia.

My mouth opened but no words came out. This was because an incredible act of fantasy reassignment was underway in the brain. Instead of the willowy woman of my dreams, Olivia had turned out to be an Audrey Hepburn lookalike.

Could I like her? I asked. Oh, you bet! came the reply.

'Yes, I am,' I said, beaming. That was the moment when I noticed a man lurking behind, tall and gangling and bespectacled. He was, I immediately guessed, the boyfriend, a figure I had typically not included when, over the preceding weeks, I had imagined this evening.

'This is Declan,' said Olivia, embracing the etiolated love object. 'He's also the society president.' I shook my rival's hand.

The next part of the evening was a blur. I had a drink and made small talk. The room filled as fifty members showed up, mainly lusty men and girls from the west of Ireland. Among these was the society's treasurer, a lantern-jawed behemoth called Keith. As we were introduced I couldn't help noticing that Keith refused to acknowledge either Olivia or Declan and that no sooner had he finished shaking my hand but he darted off.

'My ex,' whispered Olivia.

Of course, ex-boyfriends hadn't been part of my picture of the evening any more than boyfriends had.

'Oh, right,' I said grimly.

We adjourned to the Limerick Lounge. I sat at the back. The members sat in rows with their backs to me. The committee, Olivia, Declan, Keith and two or three others, sat behind a table at the front facing us. Olivia had said there'd be a few minutes of business and then she'd call me down. I leafed through the manuscript of the story I had brought to read. It was about an incident in the west of Ireland in my childhood.

The meeting opened. Declan said something. Keith sniped viciously at him. Members hissed. Declan called for calm, adding, 'It's nobody's business but ours.' What must have happened, I now realized, was that her loveliness had only recently switched from Keith to Declan. The two love rivals had murder in their hearts, feelings shared by several members on the floor.

The rhetoric got nastier. I tried to slide away but Olivia caught my eye and signalled the end of this ordeal was imminent. I bolted for the door but she ran down and stopped me before I could leave. Finally, after what seemed like an eternity but was actually an hour of procedural hideousness, I stood. I sensed, correctly, no one wanted to hear me. Panic surged in my gut. Instead of going to the front I blurted out the first sentence to the backs of the heads before me.

Well, now I'd started, I thought, I'd best continue. I remembered the advice of my speech teacher. When reading aloud, pick someone in the audience and read to them. If they're captivated, so will everyone else be.

There was no difficulty deciding to whom to read from among the members of the committee facing me. I locked my sights on Olivia and read on. She did not disappoint. Her liquid eyes looked back at me, full of attention and interest.

I was winning, I thought. I could win them round. I could make them listen.

Pride, as we know, comes before a fall. In the crowd, I could feel a change in mood. Something was going on. At first I couldn't tell what it was or where it was happening. Then I saw. Keith had silently moved his seat back from the committee table to a place his rival couldn't see him and he was now, dumb-show fashion, satirically re-enacting intercourse between the diminutive Olivia and the stringy Declan. This involved some ugly finger work. Suddenly, alerted by the tittering, Declan twigged. He turned and, realizing he'd been mocked and by whom, he picked up the glass in front of him, and threw its contents in Keith's face. The sodden treasurer smirked and muttered, 'You eejit.'

I broke off from the story and said, 'Do you want me to finish?'

'Not really,' said one voice.

'No we fucking don't,' said another.

A third was making mock farting noises.

For a second I contemplated saying something nasty, and then running out, hopefully with Olivia in tow. But she was holding Declan's hand while giving Keith, who was wiping his face with a handkerchief, the finger. No, clearly discretion was the better part of valour here. I stuffed the manuscript of the story into my pocket and fled through the doors, across the bar and out into the street.

I never did get paid.

'Silence is the unbearable repartee.' G.K. Chesterton

Billy Collins

While on a recent trip to England to promote a new book of my poems, I was presented with a rare cultural opportunity. I was invited to join the British Poet Laureate (I like to insist on the capitalized form) in a video link-up to a literary festival in Aberdeen. Not only would the two Poets Laureate – the preferred plural – from Britain and the United States be brought together for the first time to read their poetry and discuss the poetic issues of the day, which were bound to range interestingly from the aesthetic to the political, but our poetry and opinions would be presented in a truly high-tech fashion. The plan was that on a Friday evening, Andrew Motion and I would meet in a studio in London and through the magic of satellite whatever, our images would appear on a huge screen in Aberdeen before a crowd of eager poetry lovers who would see the occasion not only as the highlight of the literary festival they were attending, but as a chance to be a small part of something truly historical. A thing unprecedented in the chronicles of British–American cultural relations, a tale for the grandkids on a winter's evening.

I was personally excited at the prospect and grateful to our host in Aberdeen who had concocted the idea and made all the technical arrangements. Earlier that week I had given a few poetry readings and been the subject of a number of inter-views, but such events were familiar rituals in what had become my life in poetry. In fact, I had been performing so often that I had lately begun to feel that I was on display, a bit like a go-go dancer only without the cage and the white boots and, of course, the dancing itself. But this – an inter-country video link-up with the only two living national Poets Laureate – this was a thing quite out of the ordinary.

Looking back on it, I see that my expectations had been pitched somewhat too high. That the building to which I was escorted by a very attractive publicist was known as the 'Cruci-form Building' was the first hint that a measure of pain might be involved. The studio itself was a small, fiercely lit room with a long news desk which faced two television sets atop which sat the large, glassy, monitorial eye of a camera. One screen would show our faces in the studio, and the other would show the crowd at Aberdeen. In the room there were posters advertising our books and actual books displayed on the desk but no Andrew Motion. I sat uncomfortably behind the desk examining my tired-looking face on one television while a discussion ensued among the publicists and tech-nicians about whether to display the books in a neat stack or a casual sprawl. Assured by one technician that we were on 'mute' so the Aberdeen audience could not hear us, I uttered a few potentially disastrous, ugly-American things like 'Say what part of Wales is Aberdeen in, anyway?' just to pass the time. Finally, my fellow Laureate arrived, just in the nick.

Hands were shaken, seats were taken, and then there
appeared on the second screen the face of our moderator/host
in Aberdeen, the warm and enthusiastic Alan Spence. The
link-up was at last linked-up. Trouble was that the quality
of the video picture was awful. The image was very fuzzy,
reminiscent of a TV picture from the 1950s when the rabbit's
ears required constant readjustment. Plus, the image was often
broken up into segments like pictures from a space capsule.
At one point in the camera's explorations, the moderator
looked like a fully dressed, male version of 'Nude Descending
a Staircase'. And there was no sound, just his lips moving.
When the sound did come on, he offered to give us a video-
look at the venue. Somehow, I had expected an outdoor scene,
like Woodstock or the Monterey Jazz Festival, or Slane Castle,
but the scene was a huge classroom auditorium – a classroom
that had every appearance of being empty.

'We're going to let the crowd in any minute,' the moderator
said, and I pictured them pressing against the doors, being
restrained by heavy-set ushers. But when 'any minute' arrived,
we were again given a long shot of the venue. A few people
were making their way very slowly down the aisles, very
slowly and very few. The rough count that I made in the
course of the broadcast was twenty-three. They seemed to be
mostly elderly women, though that impression may have been
the result of all the fuzz. They were sitting as far from one
another as the room would allow – as if there had been a
terrible falling-out in the mini-bus that brought them all here.

Well, I read some poems, then Andrew Motion read some
poems, but because we were reading to an absentee audience,
to a television screen really, a dead feeling pervaded the
experience. It was as if Mr Motion and I had decided to spend
the evening together watching television – one for each

because we could never agree on a programme – and then we suddenly broke into poetry. Never had I experienced such an absence of feedback. Then our astronaut/moderator called for questions from the audience. Pause. No questions. 'Surely, one of you . . .' A silence descended, the kind of silence that Scotland may be said to be famous for. But after some genial words were traded back and forth between the Laureates in London and the moderator floating in outer space, two of the more curious audience members had questions. For Mr Motion. None for me. A final exchange revealed that it was now raining in both London and Aberdeen.

What I will never forget about the evening is staring at the fuzzy screen about halfway through the programme and noticing a figure in black getting up and walking out, right up the middle aisle of the auditorium and out the door, reducing the audience by 1/23rd. The figure in black seemed to be a woman, and I was sorely tempted to yell out from the big screen like Big Brother, 'Hey you! In the black! Get back to your seat or you will be taken to a room not of your liking.' I was restrained only by my suspicion that the figure could be my good friend, the novelist and festival-goer Todd McEwen, passing silent judgment on the whole affair and, for that matter, the very purpose of poetry.

'Better a red face than a black heart.' Portuguese proverb

Ciaran Carson

I was in Berlin in 1991, at the invitation of Jürgen Schneider and
Thomas Wolfhart of LiteraturWERKstatt. The name – meaning
something like Literature Workplace, I suppose, with the
emphasis on WORK, was vaguely off-putting, but my misgivings were allayed when Jürgen and Thomas arrived in
Belfast to check out the literary scene. Gaunt, pale, dressed
all in black, they conducted themselves with a laconic intensity that seemed the epitome of urban radical literary chic. It
turned out they knew people in Belfast I didn't know. I was
impressed.

And when the time came, I was delighted to be in Berlin.
LiteraturWERKstatt was situated in Pankow, a suburb of East
Berlin, in a mansion which had been a former Communist
Party redoubt. The Wall had been down for two years, but
the East was still intriguingly dark, and revolution was still
in the air. The bars were pleasantly dark and musak-less. They
served two kinds of beer and two of schnapps. The days were
full of drink and smoke and talk, of hope and poetry and

politics. Literature mattered. Being from Belfast, I was made
to feel special. I represented a tough, uncompromisingly urban
poetry. Exploring the gritty, dark, semi-derelict zones near the
centre, I felt charged with the street wisdom of our divided
cities. I saw Belfast in Berlin, and Berlin in Belfast.

On the third day I walked alone through the Brandenburg
Gate into the West. After a while I found myself on a thorough-
fare, where a group of people had gathered around some kind
of street performance. It turned out to be a variant of the old
three-card trick, or Find the Lady, where the punter has to
guess which of three face-down cards is the queen, and the
obvious choice is always wrong. More specifically, it was a
kind of thimblerig, where a pea is placed under one of three
thimbles. In this case, matchbox trays replaced the thimbles.
Now, I was from Belfast, and I was nobody's mug. I watched
the proceedings with a cold ironic eye, pitying the poor saps
who fell for such an ancient scam. The rig was worked by
two Turks. I watched the thimblerigger's deft movements, his
accomplice scanning the crowd for potential victims. It was
really quite an entertaining show. I observed that some of the
punters guessed right, and went off happily clutching a fistful
of marks. Of course they were in on the scam, too. But then
again, as I watched closer, and longer, every so often there
was a winner who looked nothing like the disreputable types
who made up most of the winners. These were solid-looking
Germans, family men. Even the odd respectably dressed
woman. It appeared that the thimblerig operators had worked
up a really good scam, one in which there were, *pour encourager
les autres*, genuine winners. So I watched for an even longer
time until I knew I had worked out the pattern, the moves
that would precede a win, when the pea was under the box
that everyone thought it was under. My moment came.

Quickly, before anyone else could bet, I walked boldly forward from the crowd and held up a few notes.

'Not enough,' said the Turk. He had very good English. Not only that, he knew me for an English speaker before I'd opened my mouth. 'You are sure. You know the box. You give me more. Make it worth your while.'

Not unwillingly, I gave him more. The equivalent, I think, of about eighty pounds sterling. After all, I *was* sure. I was Belfast streetwise, good enough for anything Berlin could throw up. Asking me for more was just a way of diverting my attention. So I never let the box with the pea under it out of my sight. I gave him the money and pointed.

The other Turk flipped over the box. There was nothing there. He lifted an adjacent box to reveal the pea. I stared for a few seconds in disbelief. Then, cheeks burning with shame as I realized the Turks must have seen me coming, had noticed my attention from the first moment I had set foot in the circle, had drawn me in hook, line and sinker, I walked away.

In retrospect, I consoled myself with the fact that I had witnessed an artistic performance of the highest quality. In fact, when you looked at it in the proper light, I had done no more than donate an honorarium to a group of fellow artists. I was being paid for being in Berlin, after all. Here was an authentic WERKstatt, real street theatre, in which my disbelief had been successfully – and comically, I had to agree – suspended. Was it not right that I should pay a tithe to these people, so admirably living off their wits?

Therein lay the Turks' real triumph.

'All poets are mad.' Robert Burton

Michael Donaghy

Plato warned that poets are powerless to indite a verse or chant an oracle until they are put out of their senses so that their minds are no longer in them, and ever since no one feels entirely comfortable sharing a cab with one. In fact, a cabbie once pulled over and ordered me out when my travelling companion introduced me as a poet. Incredible? Mind you, my friend had just introduced himself as 'a philosopher'. Normal people don't want to hear that sort of thing. But I'm sure it wasn't always as humiliating as it has been in these days of professionalism, promotion and 'bringing poetry to the people', running after them imploring *Come back! It doesn't have to rhyme!* The Moderns were dignified, right? Apart from Edith Sitwell's turban, I mean. Tell me Yeats got a bit of diced swede stuck in his ear dodging a food fight on an Arvon Schools course. Tell me Pound saw his photo in the local *Advertiser* under the headline RHYMESTER EZ SEZ POETRY IS EASY AND FUN. Up until the end of the war Pound thought humiliation meant having to work in a bank. I guess public readings have changed everything.

Take the case of Dylan Thomas. But there's a class/gender issue there. Sure, many (most?) poets take a drink, often to legendary excess. But name me three working-class male poets not already in AA who don't routinely douse their brains out after every reading. And oh, afterwards! The waking up still drunk next to a strange woman, waking up next to a man, or an animal! Waking up beside a strange dead male animal in a pool of ... well, in a pool. And *teaching* poetry! Coaching your students in the finer points of rhetoric and prosody so they too can experience the misspelled rejection slips, the personally inscribed copies of their books in the charity shop, the reading fee consisting of the festival souvenir mug and book token, the laid-on meal at McDonald's, the floor spots who make up half the audience and who all leave before – no – during your first poem, and the MC who introduces you as Matthew Sweeney. Twice. And best of all, the waking up alone in the middle of the night biting and tearing at the sweaty hotel sheets whimpering no no no.

Am I confusing the humiliations visited upon poets with the humiliations poets create for themselves? The business already provides plenty without any help from me so I no longer mix drink and verse. Not much. But I used to put away a bottle of vodka during my readings. It wasn't nerves. It was shame. I'd secretly fill the regulation pitcher by the lectern and appear to be knocking back water after every poem. As you do. But drink only ever made things worse. Once after reading at the Poetry Society I saw a pattern of pages laid out on the bookshop floor where a member of staff had been painstakingly collating his concrete poem consisting of large bar codes. I'm told I blurted something about *hopscotch*, broke free of the friends who were carrying me to the door, and executed what was later described to me as 'an ape dance' all over his efforts.[1] I remember the shock turning to rage on his face as I slowly realized what I'd done. He would *not* forgive me, though I hung from his lapels weeping, pleading with him to accept my apology. I had subjected myself to another indignity. As for the concrete poet, I was the indignity poetry had inflicted upon him. In *Keats and Embarrassment*, a book I was once caught out pretending to have read, Christopher Ricks suggests that indignation drives out embarrassment, *one hot flush drives out the other, as fire fire*. And speaking of driving, a generous arts officer once gave me a lift back to the station the morning after a reading and for her kindness watched me sicken, open her car door, miss the tarmac, and fill the map pocket, drowning her *Leeds A-Z* in an acid indigo porridge of red wine, Jameson's and aubergine curry. Many years passed before I was invited back to Leeds. And once I was sick on Paul Farley. He *forgave* me. People do. That's the worst part, isn't it? Phoning round the next day to grovel and being told 'No no, you were *charming!*'

You were charming, darling, because you slotted into a little niche in the cliché centre of the brain. You impish rogue, you. You dangerous firebrand, you. You profound sage, you consumptive aesthete, you holy fool. You silly ponce. *Get out of my cab.*

---

[1] Years later I turned a corner in a friend's house and accidentally stepped on a newly completed stained-glass window which had been laid on the floor for a moment just prior to installation. It had taken a year to make. Why am I telling you this?

'I'm all in favour of free expression provided it's kept rigidly under control.' Alan Bennett

Thom Gunn

I could start with the reading at Yale in the 1970s, where I was met by two affable undergraduates, explaining to me that the tutor who had asked me there was so busy running for political office that he had deputized the task of meeting me to them. Unfortunately he had not remembered to advertise the reading itself, so when I gave it later, in the corner of a library, there were only three to the audience. But they were the two sturdy undergraduates joined by somebody I recognized at once must be Holly Stevens, from her similarity to the famous picture of her father on the cover of his *Collected Poems*. That compensated for my mortification, and my vanity kept up very well.

Everybody has had such an experience, or worse. (I know one poet who flew all the way from San Francisco to the Mid-West to give a reading where *nobody* turned up.)

Fast-forward to Chicago, October, 1995. I had been unwise enough to write a sequence of songs to be sung, in a hypothetical opera, by Jeffrey Dahmer. He was the famous mass-murderer who sodomized his victims and then ate them. I thought that if Shakespeare could undertake an examination of such a man in *Macbeth*, then I could try to do it with Dahmer.

Even more unwisely, I started the reading with all five poems. As soon as I had finished them, a number of old ladies sitting together in the front row simultaneously rose and started to leave. I thought I ought to address their backs as they climbed the steps out of the auditorium. 'I am sorry I upset you ladies,' I said, 'but if I had written a poem to be spoken by Napoleon or Julius Caesar you wouldn't have thought anything of it. They killed millions more people, and at least Jeffrey Dahmer enjoyed *his* victims.' (I said this, or I think I said it. It is on tape somewhere.) They continued to climb the steps, and none so much as looked around before leaving. I remember each of them as identical, rather like Baudelaire's hallucinatory old men, each of them the same age. (They were probably not as old as I was, already in my sixties.) A multitude of thoughts hit me: had they foreseen that I might read the distasteful poems, which they already knew from my book three years earlier, and thus sat in the front row with the intention of walking out, so as to teach me a lesson? Was it spontaneous, Matrons of Chicago? Probably my remark about his enjoyment didn't help at all. Perhaps, after all, it was not mortifying but rather splendid that I had finally succeeded in offending people after having tried unsuccessfully to do so all my life.

Or on the other hand, perhaps they were just bored.

'Writing in English is the most ingenious torture ever devised for sins committed in previous lives. The English reading public explains the reason why.' James Joyce

Alan Warner

Some time back we had just moved to a new district in a city. The unfamiliar intercom buzzed. Our next-door neighbours had called round with a package which the postie had been unable to deliver. Middle-aged, busy, pleasant, our neighbours were quick to tell us they were renting 'between homes'. I liked them but was a little surprised when both came round with what was a small parcel.

To my horror the gentleman said, 'We hear you're a writer!?'

'Exciting!' the lady added.

Our shared landlord had blabbed. I'd had to confess the truth of my dark trade to him in the course of proving I was vaguely creditworthy.

For ten days or so, there were polite words at the wheely bin, the odd wave as the neighbours drove off in their car.

One evening the intercom buzzed again. I leaped up. I'd been relaxing with a few beers. After a hard day in the pub having a few beers. Our neighbours were at the door again, clutching another delivery: the immediately familiar cardboard packaging of Amazon.com. My stomach sank but I invited them into the hallway. They would come no further.

'You must be SO busy. We've got a little something we hoped you'd just quickly *autograph* for us.'

I immediately blustered that they *shouldn't* have. I had copies of my books inside, a whole box of them! If they had said they were interested . . . !

The 'You shouldn't have' bit wasn't false humility. It was also because my latest novel contained a long, detailed scene of a man urinating into a willing young woman's mouth. I imagined our friendly exchanges at the wheely bin becoming a little more terse in future weeks. The battle lines of decency were being drawn up on our lane, I thought to myself smugly.

And perhaps as I look back on it, this is the reason for the mistake I made next.

I got my trusty pen at the ready.

The uninitiated always turn to the inside of the front cover whereas a book should really be autographed just below the author's name, under the 'Alan Warner' and above the title of my novel, on the right hand, second page. Our neighbour produced the book with a flourish, smiling. By *Alan Warner*, the title of the book was, *Blues Guitar Solos Made Easy*. Dear Reader, this was not a work which emanated from my own pen.

Despite not really feeling involved, I still experienced that despicable little twinge of wounded pride, the same flush of anger you try to suppress and shrug off good-humouredly, each time none of your novels is stocked in the airport shop. I also felt an unjustified distaste for my unfortunate namesake. I had actually heard of Alan Warner (II) before. Friends ordering my books off the internet had come across him and his works. As someone who had been ejected from various teenage bands for my incompetence as a guitarist, I was quickly mocked with the great irony of it all. So here I was with Alan Warner (II)'s book in my hand. I should just have laughed and told my neighbours the truth. Yet if I told them I hadn't written this book it meant they had gone to all this effort and already spent money. Now they had the wrong book they would have to go through the inscrutable means of returning it. I also felt they were kind of cute; they weren't judging me on whether I wrote this or that, they were just quite thrilled that I'd written anything at all. Did it really make any difference? Then there was the added bonus, as long as my neighbours believed I was the author of a guitar manual, they wouldn't have to stumble through scenes of vivid scatology, inventive curse words and various sexual rampages as their willow pattern teacups flew across their quaint parlour. Also, I claimed a sort of ironic and strange biographical justification. I had published a novel based on the very theme of false authorship! It was my Raskolnikov moment.

I signed the book with a confident flourish beneath another man's name. Sort of. As soon as I did it, I had the horrible thought that maybe there was an author photograph lurking somewhere in the book! The neighbours were expressing no interest at all in what I'd signed, and were in fact chatting on about recycling collections, so I feigned interest and casually turned the pages towards the back cover. Judging by Alan Warner's field of expertise, I was fearful. I expected a photo of a tubercular man with a ponytail, perhaps a tilted fedora sprouting rare bird feathers. A man ennobled with many face piercings. I began to think I too would now have to adopt such a look to live along with my lie, but hurrah! There was no author photo! Mr Warner was also the author of *Learn To Play Rock Chord Riffs*, for any neighbour, the ominously titled, *Heavy Metal Guitar Styles*, the catchy, *100 Lead Licks for Guitar* and the solid, *Beatles Guitar Intros*. I wondered if the neighbours were actually just working up to a polite request that I keep my amplifier turned down? But they chatted on amiably. I was thinking it was certainly no shame to be mistaken for Mr Warner, clearly one hell of a guitarist.

As I nodded, the husband was lifting out **another** book from the Amazon.com folder. It was the novel: *Change and the Bottom Line*. And it was by Alan Warner. But this book was not by me either! Unbelievably, it was an Alan Warner (III)!

What I'd previously taken for quaintness, I now began to marvel at as fantastic incompetence. Two books by two different authors neither of which was your next-door neighbour was quite an achievement! I mean how did these people cope at Christmas? What I'd regretted before I now was enthusiastic about. I took *Change and the Bottom Line* by Alan Warner and signed it without hesitation.

Sober morning reflection and the full enormity of my crime was clear to me. Especially when I got on the internet myself and found out what I'd put my name to. Mr Warner had produced, by all accounts, a good read of a novel. *Change and the Bottom Line* is, I quote, 'a case study, fictionally treated which addresses the business management of organizational change. Alan Warner takes the characters already established in his two earlier books *The Bottom Line* and *Beyond the Bottom Line* and sets them in a new context. Phil Morley has become CEO of a family firm in the north of England, where his main task is to change its culture so it can meet the challenges ahead. Once again he enlists the services of Training Consultant Christine Goodheart!'

A Mr Kamesh of Hyderabad thought highly of it.

I had a strange surge of empathy that the sober-seeming Mr Alan Warner (III) once may have been, or may yet be asked to autograph one of my dubious works, by an over-enthusiastic neighbour, hopeful my words will improve his organizational business skills.

The paranoia began. I knew it would be a few days before the first note came through our letter box. By that stage I wouldn't answer the intercom any more. It would be a request from our neighbours' nephew for guitar lessons. I knew it would be a matter of weeks after that when I was asked to advise on some changes being planned at my neighbours' office. Asked to come along and give a talk to the staff perhaps!

A few days later I actually had a nightmare. I was at a gruesome formal cocktail party. On my left side stood two middle-aged men in suits, grilling me on firm business practice while on my right, a youth tugged at my trousers asking for advice on heavy-metal guitar riffs. Knowing nothing about either topic I was bluffing hopelessly and they were becoming more angry at my lack of knowledge. Unable to decide what to wear for the party, when I glimpsed myself in a prominently placed dream mirror, I was dressed in an insane conglomeration of pinstripe suit, cowboy boots and a Stetson with coloured feathers.

I was saved. Before there was any reaction to the books I'd claimed authorship of, my wife broke joyous news. Our neighbours had bought a new house and were moving out in days! They had apologized. It was such a hectic time for them they had not read my books yet but they were looking forward to them. I realized even if I'd given over signed copies of my own novels, my neighbours were not readers, and those books also would have remained unopened on the shelves forever. Just goes to show: nobody reads anything any more. Thank God!

'Let us stay at home: there we are decent. Let us not go out: our defects wait for us at the door, like flies.' Jules Renard

Roddy Doyle

The room was long and narrow. I looked out the window and saw the tracks right below me, four straight lines of them. I had a look at the bathroom. One towel, hanging over the toilet bowl. I sat back on the bed, but it wasn't easy. I kept sliding on the nylon bedspread. The television was a small thing at the far end of the room. I looked for the remote control. There wasn't one. A train passed. I got off the bed and walked to the telly. A train passed. I turned it on. A train passed.

I was in Bremen. I think I was in Bremen. I was definitely in Germany.

I'd been away from home for five or six days – a city a day, a train a day, a hotel a day – and there were five or six more days to go.

The night before it had been Hamburg. The good-looking city, but the taxi kept going for five or six miles and dropped us at the Hotel Nylon, a big terraced house near nowhere. Nylon bedspread, and sheets. A grey towel in the bathroom. There were three interviews arranged for the afternoon. But only one journalist turned up, and he brought two pals with him, including one who, I found out later, had just written a bad review of the book I was talking about. The journalist took no notes and whispered a lot to his friends. They laughed softly and, now and again, they smiled at me.

The reading that night was fine, a nice, friendly crowd. Then a tour of St Pauli and the red-light district. Women in windows, teenage girls on corners, their skin grey from the cold. In a bar, on a screen above my escort's head, the same penis penetrated the same vagina for the time it took me to drink two beers, very slowly – it must have been the director's cut – while my escort knocked back Scotch and stuffed the receipts into his pocket. Then back to the Hotel Nylon, and Bremen the next day and another Hotel Nylon, and another night between nylon sheets.

A train passed. Every ten minutes. This was Germany. Coal, steel, cars, beer. All night.

But I don't blame Germany. And I don't blame my escort, although his disappointment was there in his sad, red eyes; stuck with an Irish writer who wouldn't drink with him under the table – it was in his sighs, in his disappearances and returns. But I don't blame him.

I blame myself. I should have gone home after the second day. And I blame the sheets. It was the nylon that did it. I went to bed cold, lay awake, cold, woke up, cold. Got on the wrong train; got off. Got on the right train. The escort suggested a drink. Half-ten in the morning.

No, thanks.

Silence. All the way. He went away, and came back. Went away, came back. (I remember the book I was reading. *In Europe's Name: Germany and the Divided Continent*, by Timothy Garton Ash. I took it down off a shelf a few minutes ago, and it opened at Page 208. 'The degree to which the German nation actually had been "held together" can also be overstated.' That must have been the page I read on the train to Hamburg, over and over, while my escort sighed, and went away.) Frankfurt, Hamburg, Bremen, Cologne. We got on the wrong train, twice. We missed the right train, once. We got off in the wrong town, once. Nine days, ten.

Most of the readings were fine. They even paid me for some of them. Money in brown envelopes.

Count it, please.

A few drinks with the organizers.

How are the relationships between the Irish writers and the English writers?

They're grand, thanks.

But always back to the nylon sheets. Cold floor, cold radiator. Remote control – no batteries. The grey towel that followed me all around Germany. One hotel was bang against the tracks; another, I swear to God, was on the centre of a roundabout, on the far edge of the outskirts of I can't remember where. Broken phone, no phone. Cold coffee, no coffee. The only thing warming me was my self-pity.

We walked down a street – I don't remember where; we'd an hour to kill because a journalist hadn't turned up. We passed a café. I read the name – The Writer's Café.

Will we go in for a coffee? I said.

No.

My escort had given up on me. Four days to go, maybe five. I whinged on the phone, every night. I held the hand-set out the window.

Listen.

A train passed.

What was that?

Germany's economic fuckin' miracle.

Why don't you come home?

Why didn't I?

I don't know. Loyalty to my publisher? Cowardice? Fear of the consequences? I don't know.

But, really, I do. I began to enjoy it. I woke up each morning hoping that this new day would be worse than the last one, or at least as bad. A missed train, the wrong train. A frosty silence. ('Such, then, were the sad puddles of Germanity which were all that was left, at the founding of the Federal Republic . . .': page 232 of *In Europe's Name*. There's a small coffee stain on the page. The sudden news that we were going in the wrong direction? The dash to get off? I don't remember.) An obnoxious journalist; no journalist at all. A photographer who wanted me to stand in a river and stopped talking to me when I wouldn't.

I pointed at a line on the menu.

What's this?

The bowel of the sheep.

And, always, the hotel. And, always, the sheets. I slid between them and lay there, cold, lonely, happy. This was what it was all about – this was misery, this was writing, and this was the writer's life.

It ended.

Goodbye.

Goodbye.

It was very successful, I think.

Yes. Goodbye.

Home. Three in the morning. The bed was too warm. I lay on the kitchen floor and missed Germany.

'An artist cannot speak about his art any more than a plant can discuss horticulture.' Jean Cocteau

John Lanchester

'Events', as publishers call them – readings, festivals, signings – seem to have a tropism for disaster. The audience is bored, drunk, uninterested, or simply absent; the writer is embarrassed, humiliated, under-prepared (as well as bored, drunk, uninterested or simply absent); the wrong venue is booked; the introducer pronounces your name wrong, or talks about books you haven't written, or introduces someone else; there's a fire alarm, or better still a real fire; the other person on the platform turns out to be a sworn enemy, and then after the reading has a signing queue which stretches halfway to Reykjavik while you sit there twiddling your thumbs; the copies you open to sign turn out to have already been signed. (This might seem like a small point, but to the writer it is exquisitely and instantaneously humiliating: it means these signed copies have already been returned unsold by a bookshop somewhere else. I've seen this happen twice, never thank God to me, and both times it was like someone taking a blow to the heart.)

In a sense, all these stories are the same story, and they have the same underlying cause. The truth is that the whole contemporary edifice of readings and tours and interviews and festivals is based on a mistake. The mistake is that we should want to meet the writers we admire, because there is something more to them in person than there is on the page, so that meeting them in the flesh somehow adds to the experience of reading their work. The idea is that the person is the real thing, whereas the writing is somehow an excrescence or epiphenomenon. But that's not true. The work is the real thing, and it is that to which readers should direct their attention. The writer herself is a distraction, a confusion, a mistake – she should be heard and not seen. If you want to meet her, go to meet her on the page. The failure to see this basic reality is the reason why books events are so prone to go wrong; and the melancholy truth is that even when they go right they are usually, in the words of Dave Eggers, 'aggressively boring'.

That's what I've come to believe. I feel strongly on the point – just not strongly enough to put the belief into practice. When the invitations arrive, and especially when a new book comes out, I start to feel, what the hell, is it really so bad to go and actually meet a few readers? Isn't my view that it's all a mistake just a fantasy of uncontaminated purity, a low-key version of megalomania? Everyone else does it, what's so special about me? What's the worst that can happen?

Ah yes, the worst that can happen . . . My personal worst – perhaps I should say, worst so far – was at a Waterstone's gala dinner. I was one of twelve writers whose job was to make a short speech plugging our books and then give out an award. The first writer was Henry Cooper, who after a short and funny chat with Steve Knott of Waterstone's took the microphone and told boring stories for what felt like a long time. When it came to the question of the book, he explained that he was looking forward to sitting down with his ghost.

As the other writers came and went – Murray Walker, Mel B, Gordon Banks – I began to think that it would be a good idea, when it came to my turn, to be as short and to the point as possible. Sandi Toksvig got the biggest laugh of the night when she said that 'I knew it was going to be a long evening, but I didn't expect to be accruing pension rights.' I was on after her, the ninth or tenth turn of the evening, and gave myself a strict brief: keep it short. When Steve Knott asked me to talk about my new novel, I said how pleased I was to be a Book of the Month. I said, 'It's difficult to talk about the book, having finished it.'

My feeling was that this was a concise yet subtle, humane, and not often remarked point of difficulty in the whole business of talking about your own books. I meant that it was difficult to talk too much about the book, because it was finished and done with, a completed artefact, and they are harder to discuss, I've always found, than something you are currently working on, in the way that some of the other writers here are still working on their books.

At least, that was what I meant to say. It was what I thought I was going to say when I opened my mouth. But what I actually said was, 'It's difficult to talk about the book, having written it.' I could hear a half-laugh, half-gasp. I opened my envelope and handed it over – Best Individual at Head Office, which went to the great Rupeen Anarkat in Accounts – and was halfway back to my chair through a silent and not especially smiley audience when I realized what I had done. By and large, you only get in trouble for saying things which are true: I had inadvertently implied that most of the other writers present at that evening hadn't written their own books. There was just enough truth in this remark to make it fantastically, almost hallucinogenically offensive, especially since the whole business of ghost writing is, in publishing circles, radioactive. There were about 500 people in the room, and about 300 of them were at tables occupied by people I had just grossly insulted. I had planned to make an eirenic general point with which anyone could agree, and had ended up behaving like a more than usually drunk and boorish Liam Gallagher. If I was in any doubt on the point, the next writer to present a prize was Alan Titchmarsh, and his first words on getting to the stage were (not jokily), 'I'd just like to assure John Lanchester that I wrote every single word of my book myself.'

I turned to the person on my left, Will Atkinson from Faber. 'Am I imagining things or did Alan Titchmarsh just call me an arsehole?'

'Yes.'

This happened a year ago. I have stopped thinking about it once every ten minutes and am down to thinking about it once every week or so. It still makes me groan and double over and say 'never again'. Worse things happen at sea, I suppose. But I don't work at sea.

'Only the deep sense of some deathless shame.'
John Webster, *The White Devil*

Anne Enright

I was shortlisted once for the Kerry Ingredients Listowel Writers' Week Prize for Irish Fiction. It was all a bit long for putting in a short biog, but still, I thought, this is nice: I have a few Kerry Ingredients myself; a grandfather who left Ballylongford, just up the road from Listowel, in the 1920s.

The letter said that the winner would be announced during the actual Writers' Week and they were hoping that I would make it down, but I had various deadlines and a small baby so I let the invitation slide. Then one of the organizers rang to follow the invitation up. She was really most persuasive. Although, of course, she could not, would not tell me who had won the Kerry Ingredients Listowel Writers' Week Prize for Irish Fiction, she did say how much they would be really, *really* pleased to see me there. It seemed churlish to refuse. What the hell. Even if I hadn't won, I would have a good time. And besides . . . she sounded very keen.

It is only a six-hour drive to Kerry, but I had to pack the baby up first and bring her across town to stay at my mother's, so that added another two or three and suddenly we were looking at eight, maybe nine hours and I was late already by two o'clock. I didn't stop for lunch. On the other side of Limerick I was hurtling on such a trajectory that I had forgotten where Kerry was and how you got to it, and was too busy driving to reach for the map. I wrenched myself off the road, finally, outside a shop in Adare, where I bought six cotton pillowcases and two beaded things you put over milk jugs to keep out the flies, and I asked my way to Listowel. They pointed down the road.

Actually, I don't have a milk jug. It is one of my ambitions to get beyond the litre box on the kitchen table, but I saw the perfect milk jug once and didn't buy it, so now I keep waiting until I come across it again. Also beaded bits and bobs aren't really my thing, but I think I was a little mad by now. I was late. I was starving. I was missing the baby. I wound down the windows and turned the music up high.

North Kerry is very beautiful and, as the roads got narrower, I wondered why our grandfather left this place, and what kind of man he might have been. He married a schoolteacher's daughter in County Clare and farmed the land that came with the deal. I thought of her life; the piano that ended up in the hen house, the way she called her father 'Papa', the remnants of French, the front parlour gentility and, in the middle of it all, this Kerry man who got the farm. I am not sure they got along. I passed through a village and saw 'Enright's' written over a pub façade. There would be pictures in *The Kerryman* of Listowel Writers' Week; they would lean over the bar counter and say, 'Is she one of ours?'

My ironed dress hung from its hanger, and flapped a little from the breeze in the back of the car. When *The Third Policeman* got turned down by every publisher in London, Flann

O'Brien told the old lags in the Palace Bar that he had left the manuscript on the back seat of the car, and it had blown out the window on a trip from Donegal, page by page.

How different everything was, now. I was getting quite emotional. All these various thoughts – of success and failure and greed and homecoming – were by way of avoiding making acceptance speeches in my head. Because, of course, I did not know if I had won the Kerry Ingredients Listowel Writers' Week Prize for Irish Fiction or not. Even so, it was quite a tease. There were no obvious big hitters on the list. Besides, I had done some other prizes with this book, and they didn't expect the shortlist to turn up. The Whitbread waves a few names around and then invites the winner (not me). The Encore Prize just rings you up and says 'You've won!' – fantastic. Whereas . . . the Kerry Ingredients Listowel Writers' Week Prize for Irish Fiction says, 'Please come. No really, please.'

So, as I bowled along, I tried not to draft a few modest remarks about the Kerry grandfather who came from just up the road – in which I certainly didn't mention the junked piano, or the nuptial acquisition of land. I strenuously avoided the phrase 'coming home'. I did not say that, by a strange coincidence, one of the two judges had been, for some years, my English teacher at school. Nor did I quip that she had only ever given me a C. Actually, that last bit I really kept scrubbing out of the acceptance speech that I was not writing on the roads of North Kerry. No matter how I phrased it, it seemed a little *small*. Also the bit about how she had given me a B once 'up to the last paragraph', but then a C overall because the ending was too sentimental. Nor that this essay was about summers on my grandmother's farm. Nor that this childhood essay was the foundation, in many ways, for a section of the book that had just been awarded (or not awarded) the Kerry

Ingredients Listowel Writers' Week Prize for Irish Fiction. None of this made it into the speech that I wasn't writing in my head – there was always that niggling thing that said 'She didn't like it so much in 1976 . . .' and then a niggling hope, 'It will all be set to rights, now.'

They don't give you directions to Writers' Week, because it is so easy to find. At the end of a long straight road you drive into Listowel, and you keep going until you hit a bend that turns into the town square. In the crook of that bend is the Listowel Arms Hotel. The end of the road.

My accelerator leg was shaking from nine hours pressing the pedal as I slung my dress over my arm and checked in to the hotel. The woman behind the festival desk didn't, in fact, seem really, *really* pleased to see me. She didn't seem to recognize my name, but she checked a list and told me there would be photos in fifteen minutes' time. Up in my room, I showered cold and slapped my face a bit. I put my dress on and did a big Aaah, Eeeeh, Oooh, stretching my mouth in the mirror. I looked at myself very seriously, eyeball to eyeball, then twinkled, as though sharing a secret joke with my reflection. Then I lifted my chin, and left the room.

I went down to the foyer and found my old English teacher. We shook hands and laughed at our changed circumstances and she told me that I had not, in fact, won the Kerry Ingredients Listowel Writers' Week Prize for Irish Fiction. She tried to soften the blow. She said that, in a way, I was the wrong kind of writer for the award, and probably shouldn't have been on the list at all.

The organizer came along and was delighted to see me and said that the photos were happening any minute, outside.

'Right,' I said, and I walked out into the square. Then I kept walking and sat in my car. Then I got out of my car and went into a country hardware shop and bought two plain plastic window boxes, that were really cheap and just the right size. Then I went into a toy shop and bought the baby a toy phone. I hadn't been in a shop for months. I used the change from the toy phone to ring my mother from a real phone in the square. She told me the baby was just fine. I told her I hadn't won.

'Be nice,' she said, a little frantically, as the pips started to go. 'Try. Do try to be nice to everyone, will you?'

Back in the hotel foyer the organizer, who seemed to know what was wrong, said, 'Have a drink, there's a buffet inside.' I hadn't eaten in ten hours. There was a huge crowd around the buffet, but she found me a glass of wine. I drank it and left. Two women followed me and caught me at the door of the hotel and brought me back inside to the organizer. She said, 'Please sit here. Look, here's your chair.'

I realized as I sat down that I was placed in a convenient position for going on stage. The question was, when? The evening never seemed to start. Then it did. There was a choir. Then there was a keynote speech from an intellectual with ferociously witty eyebrows. Then more choir. Then a corporate, sofa-shaped man from Kerry Ingredients, which seemed not to be, as I had thought, a company that made cake-mix, but something far more important. Then a few more speeches. Then finally, mercifully, the award ceremony began. First, the winner of the Bryan MacMahon Short Story Award was called up and handed a cheque. There were smiles and photos. Then the winner of the Eamonn Keane Full Length Play Competition bounded up. After this came the winner of the Poetry Competition; followed in quick succession by the Short Story, Humorous Essay, and Short Poem category winners in the Listowel Writers' Week Originals Competition. The winner of the An

Post/Stena Line New Writing Competition, which was open only to those living outside Ireland, had come all the way from London. The winner of The Islands Short Story or Poem Competition, which was open only to those who were islanders by birth, held the cheque up high for the photographer, who seemed to be taking his time. After this came the glowing winner of the Kerry County Council Creative Writing Competition for Youth 'under 9s' category, who recited a brilliant poem., followed by the winner of the under 12s who read another. This was followed by the under 14s, then the under 16s, then the under 18s category winners and their poems, which were all a joy. Everyone cheered them, including me, but as the evening ground on, I began to realize that I was the only person in the hall who had not won something, or was not related to someone who had won something. Even the other writer who was shortlisted for, but had not won, the K.I.L.W.W.P.F.I.F, had been given a prize in some other category – I can't quite recall which – I think it was for an Irish debut.

By the time it came, finally, to the climax of the evening I knew what I had to do. I had to go on stage and not get a prize. I didn't know what the not-prize would be until the man who didn't make cake-mix announced a 'Cross Pen'. This is a ball-point pen in a box. It is retractable. He put the box on the lectern and asked my old English teacher to say a few words about the shortlist. She cleared her throat and gathered her notes. I thought she would take this opportunity to say that I was very, deeply special but just, lamentably, not suitable for the prize this year. She didn't really. And then she called me up on stage to collect the ball-point pen. After which I turned to the audience and gave a little bow. Then we all stood there and got our picture taken.

'Left a bit,' said photographer. 'No, *left* a bit.'

After it was over, I went to the cash machine outside and came back in and hit the bar. I didn't know anybody. Besides there was a sort of smell off me of the woman who didn't get the award – people didn't quite know what I was *for*. I didn't know what I was for. A guy accosted me. He said I had a sadness in my life, he could see it. He said I drank too much, he should know, he used to be an alcoholic. Then he ordered three vodkas in a half-pint glass with some water on the side – no ice. I escaped over to a man I half knew, or knew of, a much-remaindered journalist in a bow tie who had been watching me across the room with a small smile. I told him an amusing story. I said how he knew my sister a little, then I griped a bit about the long drive, the no lunch, the fucking Cross Pen.

'Sorry?' he said, as though uncomprehending. Then he chortled (actually, really, chortled). 'Oh I *see*,' he said. 'You thought you had *won*.'

To which there was no answer really. In the morning, I went home.

'If only it were as easy to banish hunger by rubbing the belly as it is to masturbate.' Diogenes the Cynic, 4th century BC

Niall Griffiths

My first novel had been published only a few months earlier and this was to be my first reading in the town where I lived then and still in fact do. Many friends descended; people who had moved away over the years, they all returned for the night, off buses and trains and out of cars, all bearing gifts in the form of small folded wraps or bottles. Afternoon lines and cold vodka shots around the kitchen table at what was my flat and then to the pub until dark and then to the reading, which was rammed and went well, although I should have recognized the portent of embarrassment that throbbed in the air when I, being interviewed by a beautiful woman from local TV, went to tap her in a friendly way on the upper arm and accidentally caught her left breast instead. All captured on camera. But by that time my senses had been skewed some-what and I apologized and she laughed and all my returned friends and I went back to the pub. I remember, some hours later, being hunched over a toilet cistern with Ronnie, rolled-up tenners in our nostrils, whatever powder he had chopped out for us salty and grainy and glistening candy-floss pink on the porcelain a few inches below my face. We snorted simultaneously, and then until the world turned black a few more hours later it turned deep blue all through; a rich and resonant, thrumming blue.

I woke up in my bed. Or I was *woken* up by an odd sensation of being drained as all blood gushed south. Through the hang-over tangle, thorny snarl in my skull and skinprickle I could feel it, down there, a hot steel surging, straining so hard as if it was seeking to rip itself away from my own body and dart frantic around the room like a trapped bat. So tight, so stuffed, it seemed like it would explode were I to touch it. Why stimulants have this effect mystifies me; it makes no biological, evolutionary, or even spiritual sense (if indeed that contains any sense at all). That your polluted blood should urge procreation. That your harrowed heart should yearn to beat yet faster. But there it was, as always and again, making a marquee of the duvet, the deep snores of my girlfriend sounding somewhere down there and I couldn't wake her, couldn't put my puffed and crusted face all leering in hers and at least not expect her to do anything more than laugh and go back to sleep. Besides which, I could hear other snoring, further sleepy breathing from the adjoining front room; I clambered out of the bed and opened the door a crack and peeked in – four, maybe five slumbering humps on couches and the floor beneath blankets and overcoats and spare sheets. Four, maybe five separate and distinct snorings, a symphony of apnoea wheezing behind a wall of whiff – all that sweated booze and sweated chemicals and sweated sweat. I closed the door quietly, put some jeans on and was led by the bulge in them towards the bathroom, passing through the kitchen on the way where, amongst the empty bottles and full ashtrays on the table, lay a copy of my first novel and I regarded it as I passed. Ey, look at that; *I* wrote that, I did. That's me, my achievement. Aren't I clever? Aren't I good?

I still wonder why I didn't lock the bathroom door. The key was in the lock, I clearly remember looking at it and shrugging and not turning or even touching it at all. I think I probably reasoned that, to reach the bathroom from the front room, you would have to pass through the bedroom, and whoever did that would surely notice that I wasn't in the bed and deduce that I would be in the bathroom and so knock before entering. But it would've taken two seconds to lock the door. It would've been one small and simple twist of the wrist, some tiny, insignificant physical action. So why didn't I do it?

Maybe the urgency was too great. I remember feeling on the verge of snapping, a millisecond away from detonation; it was there, at centre, burning, bulging, just about to burst. Relief was an utter imperative; there *had* to be relief, and even if it meant a delay of a mere two seconds there was at that overheated moment a better thing to do with my right hand than turn a key.

But of course it's not, or not always, simple friction. Sometimes there must be stimulus, tactile or pictorial, and although I would've preferred tactile it was right then unattainable and I was hungover, my mind was flattened, all the drugs and drink had scraped the surface layer off my brain and to think, to fantasize or even remember, would have hurt it so I rummaged through the pile of damp-swollen magazines by the toilet, the old editions of *Viz* and *FourFourTwo* and *Fortean Times*. For anything, anything; any glimpse of smooth female flesh. Any muscular curve or arc. Any taut tendon or tanned skin. The need for relief was Snowdonia-sized; it choked the entire landscape.

This was a time of celebration. A time to be with my mates and drink and talk and laugh. We'd planned to take a few crates of beer down to the beach that day, build a fire, swim if it was warm enough, cook some fish and spuds in the embers and get drunk again. So if I got this small and necessary obscenity over with I could go and wake them all up with a big pot of tea and some toast. Have a quick shower and a cheeky line before going out. Start all over again.

In the pile there was a copy of some woman's magazine. There was a tagline: You Too Can Have A Bum Like Kylie's. Kylie's arse was only just becoming a big (little) thing at that time, and there it was on page twenty-four in tiny gold shorts. And there it was on page twenty-five, double-smiling from under the hem of a tiny white dress. And there it was on page twenty-six in oh my God a thong; a *thong* for fuck's sake, Kylie's arse, the curvature and tautness of it, the dimples in the muscles at either side and the way the light gleams off its brown roundness as she bends and the creamy sheen on the tanned tight skin of it oh my God there was Kylie's arse there was one flash and a tremendous groaning relief there was Ronnie's face over the top of the magazine. I was on my back and holding the mag upright on my chest with my left hand and there was Ron in the doorway, his face visible over the top of the page looking like the bloke in 'The Scream'. And just for a moment the two merged in my wetly swirling vision; Ronnie's howling face and Kylie's arse became part of the same person, a horrible hybrid. A Rolie, a Kylan; as if that arse was actually topped by that face. That shocked and horrored face all purple adjoining that perfect bum. Oh, the sickness.

And that was supposedly a time of celebration, and that's why I can't stand Kylie's arse; because it's always there, somewhere under the sun, it exists out there in the real world and whenever it appears on the telly or a tabloid it throws up that moment, repeatedly, that instant when relief became humiliation. I can never get away from it, never flee from its jeering; my face so hot you could warm your hands on a frosty morning. The goosepimpling skin. The contracting heart cowering, cringing. I mean, me and Ronnie, it was all grand with us, we got drunk by the sea that day and had a laugh about the whole thing, but I lost touch with him about a year ago yet I still see Kylie, two or three times a week, but I never look above her shoulders because I know whose face I'll see and it won't be hers, I don't even know what she looks like anymore, so I tend to focus on her arse instead as indeed the entire culture does, and base-fixated as we are on these things to ease the anguish of being alive among the emptinesses means and results in only nerves shredded, demolished, only life dying and drying to scale on the belly, only this neverstopping shame until death.

Biographies

Simon Armitage was born in 1963 and lives in Yorkshire. He has won numerous prizes for his nine collections of poetry which include *Selected Poems* and *The Universal Home Doctor* (Faber & Faber). His latest novel, *The White Stuff*, is published by Penguin in 2004. He is also a broadcaster and has written extensively for radio, television and film, and in 2003 received the Ivor Novello award for songwriting. He teaches at Manchester Metropolitan University.

Margaret Atwood was born in Ottawa in 1939, and has become Canada's most eminent novelist and poet. She has published over thirty books of fiction, poetry and critical essays. Her novels include *The Handmaid's Tale*, *Cat's Eye* and *Alias Grace*, all of which were shortlisted for the Booker Prize, and *The Blind Assassin*, which won the 2000 Booker Prize. Her books have been translated into thirty-three languages. She lives in Toronto.

Paul Bailey is the author of *At the Jerusalem* (1967) which won the Somerset Maugham Award, *Trespasses* (1970), *A Distant Likeness* (1973), *Peter Smart's Confessions* (1977), shortlisted for the Booker Prize, *Old Soldiers* (1980), *Sugar Cane* (1993) and *Uncle Rudolf* (2002). He was the first recipient of the E. M. Forster award and won a George Orwell Prize for his essay 'The Limitations of Despair'.

John Banville's latest book is *Prague Pictures: Portraits of a City* (Bloomsbury, September 2003). He lives in Dublin, and tries to avoid doing public readings.

Nicola Barker was born in Ely, Cambridgeshire, in 1966. Her work includes *Love Your Enemies* (David Higham Prize for Fiction and joint winner of the Macmillan Silver Pen Award for Fiction), *Reversed Forecast, Small Holdings, Heading Inland* (1997 John Llewellyn Rhys/*Mail on Sunday* Prize), *Five Miles From Outer Hope*, *Wide Open* (winner of the 2000 International IMPAC Dublin Literary Award) and *Behindlings*. She was recently named as one of the 20 Best Young British Novelists by Granta.

Julian Barnes is the author of nine novels. His collection of stories, *The Lemon Tree*, will appear in March 2004.

William Boyd is the author of eight novels, the most recent being *Any Human Heart*.

Michael Bracewell is the author of six novels, including *Saint Rachel* and *Perfect Tense*. He has also published two works of non-fiction: a study of Englishness in popular culture, entitled *England Is Mine*, and a selection of journalism, *The Nineties*. He contributes to *Frieze* magazine and *The Los Angeles Times*, and is currently researching a biography of the art rock group, Roxy Music.

André Brink was born in South Africa in 1935. He is the author of fourteen novels in English, including *An Instant in the Wind*, *A Dry White Season*, *A Chain of Voices*, and *The Rights of Desire*. He has won South Africa's most important literary prize, the CNA Award, three times, and has twice been shortlisted for the Booker Prize. His novels have been translated into thirty languages.

John Burnside has published eight books of poetry, including *Feast Days*, winner of the Geoffrey Faber Memorial Prize and *The Asylum Dance*, which won the Whitbread Poetry Prize. His prose work includes four novels and a collection of stories. He lives in East Fife, with his wife and son.

Ciaran Carson is the author of eight collections of poems and four works of prose. His novel, *Shamrock Tea*, was longlisted for the Booker Prize and he has won several literary awards, including the *Irish Times* Irish Literature Prize and the T. S. Eliot Prize. His translation of Dante's *Inferno* was published by Granta Books in 2002, and a book of new poems, *Breaking News*, by Gallery Press and Wake Forest University Press in 2003. He lives in Belfast.

Jonathan Coe has written the novels *What a Carve Up!*, *The House of Sleep* and *The Rotters' Club*, among others.

Billy Collins' most recent collection is *Nine Horses* (Picador, 2002). He was appointed United States Poet Laureate for 2001–2003. He lives in Westchester County, New York.

Louis de Bernières' first three novels are *The War of Don Emmanuel's Nether Parts*, *Señor Vivo and the Coca Lord* (both of which won Commonwealth Writers' Prizes) and *The Troublesome Offspring of Cardinal Guzman*. He was selected as one of the 20 Best of Young British Novelists in 1993, and *Captain Corelli's Mandolin* won the 1995 Commonwealth Writers' Prize for Best Book.

Poet **Michael Donaghy** was born in the Bronx, New York, in 1954. His most recent collections are *Dances Learned Last Night (Poems 1975–1995)* (Picador, 2000) and *Conjure* (Picador, 2000). He is a Fellow of The Royal Society of Literature.

Mark Doty's six books of poems include *My Alexandria*, which won the T. S. Eliot Prize in the UK and the National Book Critics' Circle Award in the USA. He is also the author of three books of non-fiction, among them *Heaven's Coast*, which won the PEN/Martha Albrand Prize for memoir. He lives in New York City and teaches at the University of Houston in Texas.

Roddy Doyle was born in Dublin in 1959. His first novel, *The Commitments*, was published to great critical acclaim in 1987 and was made into a very successful film by Alan Parker. *The Snapper*, published in 1990, was also made into a film. *The Van* was shortlisted for the Booker Prize and made into a film. *Paddy Clarke Ha Ha Ha*, which won the Booker Prize in 1993, is the largest-selling winner in the history of the prize.

Margaret Drabble was born in Sheffield in 1939 and educated at Newnham College, Cambridge. After a brief career as an actress with the Royal Shakespeare Company she became a full-time writer, and has published fifteen novels. The most recent is *The Seven Sisters*. She also edited the fifth edition of the *Oxford Companion to English Literature* (1985) of which a fully revised version (sixth edition) appeared in 2000. She is married to Michael Holroyd.

Geoff Dyer's books include *But Beautiful* (winner of a Somerset Maugham Prize), *Paris Trance*, *Out of Sheer Rage* (a finalist, in America, for a National Book Critics' Circle Award) and, most recently, *Yoga for People Who Can't Be Bothered to Do It*. He is a recipient of a 2003 Lannan Literary Fellowship.

Anne Enright was born in Dublin, where she now lives and works. Her short stories have appeared in *The New Yorker*, *Granta* and the *Paris Review*. Her collection, *The Portable Virgin*, won the Rooney Prize for Irish Literature. Novels include *The Wig My Father Wore* and *What Are You Like?* which won the Encore Prize and was shortlisted for the Whitbread prize. Her new novel, *The Pleasure of Eliza Lynch*, was published by Jonathan Cape in 2002.

Paul Farley has published two collections of poetry with Picador: 1998's *The Boy from the Chemist is Here to See You* won a Forward Prize and a Somerset Maugham Award; *The Ice Age* received the 2002 Whitbread Prize for Poetry. A former *Sunday Times* Young Writer of the Year, he lives in Lancashire.

Vicki Feaver was born in Nottingham in 1943. She has published two collections of poetry. *Close Relatives* (Secker, 1981) and *The Handless Maiden* (Cape, 1994) which was awarded a Heinemann Prize and shortlisted for the Forward Prize. A selection of her work is also included in the Penguin Modern Poets series. She lives on the edge of the Pentland Hills near Edinburgh.

Janice Galloway's highly acclaimed first novel, *The Trick is to Keep Breathing*, was published in 1990, since when she has won a number of prestigious literary awards, including the McVitie's Prize (for *Foreign Parts*) and the E. M. Forster Award. She has also written drama, short stories, opera and poems and has been published in seven languages. A major commission with Anne Bevan, *Rosengarden*, will appear in 2004. She has one son and lives in Glasgow.

Carlo Gébler was born in Dublin in 1954, brought up in London and now lives outside the town of Enniskillen in Northern Ireland. He occasionally makes films – *Put to the Test* won the Royal Television Society documentary award in 1999 – and otherwise he writes. His play *10 Rounds* was performed in London in 2002 and his novel *August '44* will be published in the autumn of 2003. He is married and has five children.

Niall Griffiths was born in Liverpool in 1966, and now lives in Wales. He is the author of *Grits, Sheepshagger, Kelly + Victor* and *Stump*, all published by Jonathan Cape. He is currently at work on a new novel *Wreckage* and is completing a collection of stories, *Further Education*.

Thom Gunn was born in 1929 in Gravesend and has lived since 1954 in California. His first book of poetry was *Fighting Terms* (1954) and his most recent *Boss Cupid* (2000).

Hugo Hamilton was born and grew up in Dublin. He is the author of five highly acclaimed novels, *Surrogate City, The Last Shot* and *The Love Test* (Faber), *Headbanger* and *Sad Bastard* (Secker), one collection of short stories and a memoir, *The Speckled People* (Fourth Estate). He has worked as a writer-in-residence at many leading universities, including most recently at Trinity College, Dublin. He has just returned to Ireland from a DAAD scholarship in Berlin.

David Harsent's most recent collection of poems, *Marriage*, was shortlisted for the Forward and T. S. Eliot Prizes. He is currently working on the libretto for a full-length opera for the Royal Opera House (music by Harrison Birtwistle).

Carl Hiaasen's novels include *Strip Tease*, *Basket Case* and, most recently, *Hoot*. He seldom leaves his home state of Florida, except when he is forced by ruthless publishers to go on book tours.

Michael Holroyd has written biographies of Lytton Strachey, Augustus John and Bernard Shaw, and also an autobiography, *Basil Street Blues*. he is president of the Royal Society of Literature.

A. L. Kennedy was born in the north-east of Scotland, home of mortification. She is the author of several novels and collections of short stories and also writes for the press, film, TV and stage. She is now, and will remain, thoroughly ashamed of herself.

John Lanchester was born in Hamburg in 1962. He was brought up in the Far East and educated in England. His first two novels, *The Debt to Pleasure* and *Mr Phillips*, have been translated into more than twenty languages. *Fragrant Harbour*, his most recent novel, was published in 2002. He is married with two children and lives in London.

James Lasdun's most recent book is *The Horned Man*, a novel. He was born in London and now lives with his family in upstate New York.

Jonathan Lethem is the author of six novels, including *The Fortress of Solitude*. He lives in Brooklyn, New York.

Michael Longley's most recent collection, *The Weather in Japan* (2000), won the T. S. Eliot Prize and *The Irish Times* Poetry Prize. He received the Queen's Gold Medal for Poetry in 2001 and the Wilfred Owen Award in 2003. A new collection, *Snow Water*, will be published in 2004.

Thomas Lynch's books include *Grimalkin & Other Poems*, *Still Life in Milford*, *The Undertaking*, and *Bodies in Motion and at Rest*. He lives in Milford, Michigan, and Moveen, Co. Clare.

Patrick McCabe's novels include *The Butcher Boy* (1992) which was the winner of the *Irish Times*/Aer Lingus Literature Prize, was shortlisted for the Booker Prize and was a highly acclaimed film directed by Neil Jordan, and *Breakfast on Pluto* which was shortlisted for the 1998 Booker Prize. His new novel, *Call Me the Breeze*, was published in September 2003. He lives in Sligo with his wife and two daughters.

Elizabeth McCracken's most recent publication is *Niagara Falls All Over Again*. She has been shortlisted for the National Book Award and awarded prestigious grants by the Guggenheim Foundation, amongst others. *Granta* recently counted her amongst the 20 best American writers under 40.

Val McDermid was born in Scotland. She has published eighteen crime novels, a short story collection and a non-fiction book. Her books are translated into over twenty languages and have won many awards, including the Gold Dagger, the *Los Angeles Times* Book Award and the Grand Prix des Romans d'Aventure.

Bernard MacLaverty was born in Belfast but now lives in Glasgow. He has published four collections of short stories and four novels (*Grace Notes* was shortlisted for the Booker Prize). He has written versions of his fiction for other media – radio plays, television plays, screenplays.

Duncan McLean has published fiction (*Bucket of Tongues, Bunker Man*) and non-fiction (*Lone Star Swing: On the Trail of Bob Wills and his Texas Playboys*) and written for TV, radio and theatre. He runs an off-licence in the Orkney Islands.

Glyn Maxwell's latest book of poetry is *The Nerve* (Picador, 2002). He lives in New York City, and currently teaches at Princeton and Columbia. He is Poetry Editor of the *New Republic*.

Claire Messud was born in the United States in 1966, and educated at Yale and Cambridge. her first novel, *When the World Was Steady*, was a finalist for the PEN/Faulkner Award in 1996. Her second novel, *The Last Life*, won the Encore Prize. She lives in Washington.

Karl Miller has been literary editor of the *Spectator* and the *New Statesman*, editor of the *Listener*, and founding editor of the *London Review of Books*. From 1974 to 1992 he was Lord Northcliffe Professor of Modern English Literature at University College London. Among his books are *Cockburn's Millennium*, *Double*, and two instalments of autobiography, *Rebecca's Vest* and *Dark Horses*. His life of James Hogg, *Electric Shepherd*, has just been published.

Deborah Moggach is the author of fourteen novels including *Tulip Fever, Final Demand, Porky* and *Seesaw*. She has also written two books of short stories and several TV dramas. She lives in London.

Rick Moody is the author, most recently, of a collection of stories, *Demonology*, and a memoir, *The Black Veil*.

Andrew Motion is the Poet Laureate and Professor of Creative Writing at Royal Holloway College. His most recent collection of poems is *Public Property* (2002); in 2003 he published his biographical fantasy *The Invention of Dr Cake*.

Paul Muldoon is the author, most recently, of *Moy Sand and Gravel*, for which he won the 2003 Griffin Prize for Excellence in Poetry and the Pulitzer Prize.

Julie Myerson was born in Nottingham in 1960 and is the author of *Sleepwalking*, *The Touch*, *Me and the Fatman*, *Laura Blundy* and, most recently, *Something Might Happen*. She lives in London with the writer and director Jonathan Myerson and their three children.

Edna O'Brien is the author of twenty-three books including *House of Splendid Isolation*, *Down by the River* and, most recently, *In The Forest*. She is the recipient of the American National Arts Gold Medal for Literature and an honorary member of the American Academy of Arts.

Maggie O'Farrell was born in Northern Ireland, and grew up in Wales and Scotland. She has worked as a waitress, chambermaid, cycle courier, teacher, arts administrator and journalist. She is the author of two novels, *After You'd Gone* and *My Lover's Lover*; her third, *The Distance Between Us*, will be published in spring 2004.

Andrew O'Hagan was born in Glasgow in 1968. His most recent novel is *Personality*. He recently received the E. M. Forster Award from the American Academy of Arts and Letters.

Michael Ondaatje's works include *Anil's Ghost*, *The English Patient*, *In the Skin of a Lion*, *Coming Through Slaughter*, *The Collected Works of Billy the Kid*, and his memoir, *Running in the Family*. His works of poetry include *The Cinnamon Peeler* and *Handwriting*. His most recent book is *The Conversations: Walter Murch and the Art of Editing Film*.

Sean O'Reilly was born in Derry in Northern Ireland. He has published a book of short stories, *Curfew*, and a novel, *Love and Sleep*. A new novel, *The Swing of Things*, will appear in February 2004.

Chuck Palahnuik's best-known novel to date is *Fight Club*, which was made into a major film. His other works include *Survivor*, *Invisible Monsters*, *Lullaby* and *Choke*. He lives in Portland, Oregon.

Don Paterson was born in Dundee and works as a musician and editor. He also teaches on the Creative Writing M.Litt. at St Andrews University. his most recent book of poems is *Landing Light* (Faber 2003).

D. B. C. Pierre is a British author born in Australia and raised in Mexico, the UK and USA. He has since worked in the arts in a dozen countries worldwide, finally settling in London to write his first novel, *Vernon God Little*. He is currently writing in Ireland.

Darryl Pinckney, a frequent contributor to *The New York Review of Books*, is the author of a novel, *High Cotton*.

Charles Simic has published sixteen collections of his own poetry, five books of essays, a memoir, and numerous books of translations. He has received many literary awards for his poems and translations, including the MacArthur Fellowship and the Pulitzer Prize. *Voice at 3 A.M.*, his selected and new poems, was published by Harcourt this spring.

Matthew Sweeney's most recent publications include *Selected Poems* (Cape, 2002), and a children's novel, *Fox* (Bloomsbury, 2002). A new book of poems, *Sanctuary*, is forthcoming from Cape in September 2004, and he is currently finishing a much-delayed book of stories.

Rupert Thomson is the author of six novels, *Dreams of Leaving*, *The Gates of Hell*, *Air and Fire*, *The Insult*, *Soft*, and *The Book of Revelation*. His seventh novel, *Divided Kingdom*, will be published by Bloomsbury in September 2004.

Adam Thorpe's latest novel, *No Telling*, was published by Jonathan Cape in 2003, as was his fourth poetry collection, *Nine Lessons from the Dark*. He lives in France with his wife and three children.

Colm Tóibín was born in Ireland in 1955. He is the author of the novels *The South*, which won the *Irish Times* First Novel Award 1991, *The Heather Blazing*, winner of the 1992 Encore Award, *The Story of the Night* and *The Blackwater Lightship*, shortlisted for the 1995 Booker Prize. He has also written a number of non-fiction books, including *Homage to Barcelona*. He lives in Dublin.

William Trevor was born in County Cork in 1928. He is the author of many novels, most recently *The Story of Lucy Gault*, which was shortlisted for the Man Booker Prize. In 1977 he was awarded an honorary CBE for his valuable services to literature, and in 2002 he received an honorary knighthood. He is a member of the Irish Academy of Letters and now lives in Devon.

Alan Warner is from Scotland, has lived in Ireland for six years and has written four novels: *Morvern Callar*, which was made into a feature film, *These Demented Lands*, *The Sopranos* and *The Man Who Walks* (all Vintage). A fifth novel, *The Oscillator* will be published in early 2005 by Jonathan Cape. Alan Warner was one of *Granta*'s Best of Young British Novelists 2003.

Irvine Welsh is from Edinburgh. His first novel, *Trainspotting*, was published in 1993. Since then he has written a collection of stories, *The Acid House*, a number of film and drama projects, and five further novels, most recently *Porno* (2002) which is being filmed. He currently lives in San Francisco.

Louise Welsh was born in London in 1965 and read history at Glasgow University, and completed an M.Litt. at Strathclyde and Glasgow University. She spent much of the last ten years as a bookseller in Glasgow. Her first novel, *The Cutting Room*, was nominated for the *Guardian* First Book Award, won the CWA John Creasey Memorial Dagger, the Robert Louis Stevenson Memorial Award and jointly won the 2002 Saltire Scottish Book of the Year Award. She lives in Glasgow.

Hugo Williams was born in 1942. He writes the Freelance column in the *Times Literary Supplement*. His *Collected Poems* were published by Faber in 2002. *No Particular Place to Go* is reprinted by Gibson Square Books.

John Hartley Williams has published eight collections of poetry. His last collection was *Spending Time with Walter* (Cape, 2001). A romance, *Mystery in Spiderville*, was reissued by Vintage in 2003. His most recent publication is *North Sea Improvisation* – available from the poet at www.johnhartleywilliams.de

James Wood was born in 1965. He has received acclaim as one of the most prominent critics of his generation. From 1991 to 1995 he was Chief Literary Critic of the *Guardian*, in London, and since then has been a Senior Editor of the *New Republic* in Washington DC. His reviews and essays appear regularly in that magazine, in the *New Yorker* and the *London Review of Books*. He has published one novel, *The Book Against God*, and a collection of essays, *The Broken Estate*; a second collection, *The Irresponsible Self*, will appear in 2004.